W9-BPM-813

HOME COOKING

With KATE McDERMOTT

HOME COOKING

With KATE McDERMOTT

photographs by
ANDREW SCRIVANI

THE COUNTRYMAN PRESS
A division of W. W. Norton & Company
Independent Publishers Since 1923

For information about permission to reproduce selections from this
book, write to Permissions, The Countryman Press,
500 Fifth Avenue, New York, NY 10110

For information about special discounts for bulk purchases,
please contact W. W. NortonSpecial Sales
at specialsales@wwnorton.com or 800-233-4830

Manufacturing by RR Donnelley, Shenzhen
Book design by Nick Caruso Design
Production manager: Devon Zahn

The Countryman Press
www.countrymanpress.com

A division of W. W. Norton & Company, Inc.
500 Fifth Avenue, New York, NY 10110
www.wwnorton.com

978-1-68268-241-8

10 9 8 7 6 5 4 3 2 1

For my grandmother, Vesta,
my mother, Louise,
and my daughter, Sara.

Contents

Introduction

You can do this. You can make any and every recipe in this book. They are not anything remotely resembling *haute cuisine*, *haute couture*, or *haute* anything. There are plenty of wonderful and inspiring recipe collections at the bookstore to help you with that. If you are looking for quick, satisfying recipes, for mainly one-dish meals, to please even the pickiest of eaters, then you've come to the right place. These are my family recipes that, even as an empty-nester, I continue to make. Now, it is my joy to share them with you.

Home cooked, home baked, homegrown, homemade. The love of tasty food, made from scratch, is one we all share, but facing a complicated multi-step recipe at the end of the day, no matter how delicious it promises to be, can be overwhelming. With a resigned sigh, we place the recipe book back on the shelf, promising ourselves that we will make it another day when we have more time. During the busy years of raising my family and working more than full time to pay the bills, I looked forward to times when I could spend hours creating in the kitchen, but truthfully days like that didn't come often. Instead of giving up, I turned to easy and tasty recipes that I could put on the table quickly, just like my grandmother and mom did. I learned that recipes, such as soups, stews, and dips, are easy to double and freeze for extra-busy days. Setting a container to defrost in the fridge the night before means we can get a homemade meal on the table F-A-S-T.

As for kitchen gear and ingredients? Nothing fancy is required here either. Your essential pieces of equipment are a frying pan, soup pot with lid, baking dish, measuring cups and spoons, cutting board, sharp knife, mixing bowl, big spoon, and spatula. A food processor is nice, but certainly not required. I learned to cook without one. Ingredients and seasonings are ones that you will find at most every grocery store. I use salted butter, whole or 2% milk, large or extra large eggs, extra virgin olive oil, and granulated sugar. Standard and metric measurements are given for each recipe, too.

I always suggest making a new recipe one time as written before changing it up, especially if you are a newbie to cooking and baking. That being said, I would be remiss if I didn't tell you that I have had some very good results putting in a bit less than a full cup of carrots, a few extra chopped onions, or a heaping instead of flat teaspoon of seasoning. If you like the results, then make a note in the margin for the next time so these recipes will become yours.

As we cook through these pages together, let the walls between our kitchens disappear, and as we share the table with our family and friends, let our bowls be filled with love.

Now let's begin.

Greg's Granola, page 30

Simple Breakfasts to Start the Day

Chapter One

"Every morning is a different painting."

Morning

I pull myself out of a warm bed and my feet find the slippers I set there the night before. It's not quite light and I pad out to the living room to see what kind of sky awaits; cloudy and gray with mist and rain, or the promise of a sunrise that shoots in my east-facing windows in breathtaking shades of magenta and gold. Every morning is a different painting. If the coals in the wood stove have held overnight, a few dry sticks are all that is needed to rekindle the flame. The crackling of wood, a familiar melody to me, breaks the stillness.

Into the kitchen now to set the kettle on the stove, I hear the click of my sweet dog's nails on the wood floor. While I prepare her food, she performs a joyful morning dance. My cat rubs up against my legs and seems to wonder what all the commotion is about. I pull out the electric grinder, which came from a church rummage sale for fifty cents, and grind my beans. More than the mug full of hot brew that will warm my hands, I love the smell of fresh-ground coffee. Like the first morning chimes of a clock, I hear the voices of the neighborhood children as they wait for the school bus just outside my fence. I remember the daily bustle of making sure my two children, Sara and Duncan, were dressed, fed, and readied to catch it, too.

Sun above the horizon now, the prism in the window puts a show of rainbow colors on the wall. Another log goes on the fire. I bring my nose closer to the rim of my mug, and inhale the memories of family breakfasts and sweet times.

Scrambled Eggs with Curry, Avocado, and Goat Cheese

I can't remember the first time I was inspired to add curry powder, avocado, and goat cheese to my breakfast eggs, but I've been making them this way for so long that they have become one of the signature breakfasts in my kitchen. They are really good served with slices of baked bacon (see Baked Up Bacon, page 24), hot buttered toast, and fresh squeezed orange juice.

SERVES 1

INGREDIENTS

2 to 3 large eggs

Pinch of salt

½ teaspoon curry powder

¼ ripe avocado per person

1 to 2 tablespoons (15 to 30 g) goat cheese or cream cheese

A teaspoon-size pat of butter

PROCEDURE

1. Crack the eggs into a bowl and fork beat until blended. Add salt and curry powder, and fork beat again. Don't worry if the curry powder doesn't mix in completely. Set aside.
2. Chop or slice avocado into pieces, and break up cheese into smaller pieces, and set aside.
3. Turn heat to medium low and heat skillet. Add a pat of butter. When butter has melted, turn the heat up to medium, and add eggs.
4. Stir with a large spoon, scraping up the egg curds from the bottom and sides. When the eggs are almost set, turn off the heat and fold in the avocado and cheese.

Greens, Garlic, and Eggs

When an unexpected friend comes over, this is a quick and easy meal. At Pie Cottage, I make it for breakfast, lunch, and sometimes supper. In the Pacific Northwest, the climate allows me to grow garden greens nearly year round and I get a wonderful feeling when walking out the kitchen door to pick a fresh basketful. All of us have busy lives, so please don't worry if you aren't growing your own greens. When you shop for them at your farmers' market or in the grocery produce section, look for the perkiest ones.

SERVES 4

INGREDIENTS

1 large bunch chard, kale, or collard greens, or a mixture of all

2 tablespoons (30 ml) olive oil

4 to 8 cloves garlic, chopped

1 medium onion, chopped small (optional)

8 large eggs

Salt and freshly ground black pepper

Balsamic vinegar

Marinated red peppers (optional)

PROCEDURE

1. Remove the leaves from the tough ribs of the chard, kale, and/or collard greens, and chop or tear into small- to medium-size pieces.
2. Heat the oil over medium heat in a large lidded skillet. If you don't have a lid, a tightly fitted piece of foil will do just fine.
3. Sauté the garlic and optional onion for a minute or two. Be careful not to burn the garlic.
4. Add the greens and stir them around to coat with the oil. Cover the pan and let cook for about 2 minutes to wilt a bit.
5. Make eight small hollows in the greens with the back of a spoon. Carefully break an egg into each hollow.
6. Pour in a few tablespoons of water. Cover the pan. Turn up the heat to medium high and let the eggs steam for 2 to 3 minutes.
7. Lift the lid and see if the eggs are done. The whites should be set. If the yolks seem too loose, put the lid back on and cook for another minute.
8. Season with salt and pepper, sprinkle some balsamic vinegar over the top, and add a few optional red peppers.

Note My favorite peppers are Mama Lil's Pickled Mildly Spicy Peppers with Garlic in Oil.

Truck Stop Café

Like many families, we liked to play "restaurant" at home. Our one-table establishment had a toy semi-truck centerpiece, with the words "Truck Stop Café" neatly printed on the side of its trailer. My son, Duncan, was the café's proprietor, waiter, and, with a little help from me, chef du jour. When the café was open, Monsieur Duncan, the smiling maître d', greeted and seated us. The café was known best for its breakfasts, and our young water listed off the daily specials. "Bacon, oatmeal, pancakes, scones, cocoa, juice . . . and how would you like your eggs today?"

Once we had agreed on our family-style order, we put on aprons and became the cooks. We squeezed fresh orange juice, cracked eggs, cooked up bacon, and, if time allowed, baked muffins or a coffee cake. Then we sat down to enjoy one of the real home-cooked meals for which the café was known. Full and satisfied, we pushed our chairs back from the table. Monsieur Duncan thanked us for coming and bid us adieu. Of course, we asked him to please give our compliments to the chef. The café has been closed for years, but someday I hope very much that it might reopen—this time run by my future grandchildren.

Duncan's Breakfast Hash, page 18

Duncan's Breakfast Hash

My son's delicious breakfast hash has quite a following among our family and friends. When he's home, it's not unusual for him to hand me a bowl first thing in the morning along with a mug of coffee. He uses two skillets, one for the onions and one for the potatoes, so that both can be done about the same time, and then mixed together with the bacon and sausage. If you only have one skillet, work in stages, and mix everything together at the end. This recipe makes a bunch, so you'll have plenty of leftovers to reheat for lunch or dinner.

SERVES 8 TO 10

INGREDIENTS

6 slices bacon

1 pound (450 g) ground sausage

¼ cup (60 ml) olive oil, plus 2 tablespoons (30 ml) for cooking

1 to 2 onions, chopped

8 big red potatoes, unpeeled and chopped in ½-inch (1-cm) dice

1 entire head of garlic, peeled and chopped small

1 teaspoon salt

¾ teaspoon freshly ground black pepper

4 scallions, whites and greens, thinly sliced

1 ripe avocado, sliced

1 handful cilantro, chopped

Hot sauce or salsa of choice

Shake the Garlic Here's an easy way to remove the skins from an entire head of garlic quickly and easily. You'll need two medium-size metal bowls. Break apart the garlic cloves and place them in one of the bowls. Place the other bowl on top. Hold the rims of the bowls together securely with both hands, and shake vigorously for a full minute. It will sound like a loud percussion section. Lift the top bowl off and you'll see that most of the skins have loosened and fallen off the individual cloves. If any skins remain, just put the lid back on and shake again. If you like, play some lively music and dance around the kitchen while shaking the bowls.

1. Cook the bacon in a large cast-iron skillet slowly over medium-low heat. Turn the bacon occasionally so that it browns evenly. Remove from pan and set aside. When cool enough to handle, cut or crumble into smaller, bite-size pieces.

2. Crumble the sausage into the pan and cook over medium heat. Flip the sausage over and continue cooking until the meat browns. Remove from pan and set aside.

3. Heat 2 tablespoons (30 ml) olive oil in a large cast-iron skillet over medium heat. Add onions and sauté until soft and translucent. Remove from pan and set aside.

4. In another skillet, heat ¼ cup (60 ml) olive oil over high heat. Cover the bottom of the pan with the potatoes and cook. Flip the potatoes with a spatula every few minutes.

5. Add the garlic about 15 minutes into cooking the potatoes. If you add it earlier, it may burn. Keep cooking the potatoes, adding more oil as needed, until they have reduced in size by about half and are crispy and golden brown on the bottom.

6. Mix the onions, salt, and pepper into the potatoes, and stir to mix well.

7. Add the bacon and sausage to the potatoes and stir. Cook a few more minutes to heat through. Add sliced scallions just before serving.

8. Serve topped with eggs cooked to order, sliced avocado, cilantro, and hot sauce or salsa.

Coddled Eggs with Herbs, page 22

Coddled Eggs with Herbs

Why oh why did I think I no longer needed my mom's vintage egg coddlers? Her classic white porcelain pieces were painted with colorful fruit, berries, and flowers, and would have been perfect for this recipe. I truly hope that whoever has them now is using them, and that they aren't hidden away on the top shelf of a kitchen cupboard, or retired to an attic. Since I didn't keep them, individual-size heatproof glass bowls, or half-pint canning jars, will work fine with this recipe, though not quite as charming a way to brighten up the breakfast table. These eggs can be easily flavored with different herbs. Rosemary leaves are one of my favorites, but oregano, marjoram, summer savory, thyme, chopped parsley, or chives are all good. It only takes a few tiny leaves to infuse flavor through the eggs. Serve with a piece of buttered toast for dipping into the yolk.

SERVES 1

INGREDIENTS

Butter

½ teaspoon heavy cream in each bowl

1 to 2 large eggs per person

Salt and freshly ground black pepper

A few leaves of fresh or dried herbs of your choice

PROCEDURE

1. Place individual-size, heatproof glass bowls in a lidded metal skillet or braising pan. Fill skillet or pan with enough water to come up to about ¾ of the way on the side of the bowls. Before heating the water, remove the bowls from the pan. Bring the water to a gentle boil over medium heat. If you cover the pan it will boil faster.

2. Grease the individual bowls liberally with butter and add ½ teaspoon heavy cream to each bowl.

3. Break 1 to 2 eggs in each bowl, sprinkle with salt and pepper, and top with 2 or 3 leaves of an herb of your choice.

4. Turn off the heat and carefully return the egg-filled bowls to the pan, cover with lid, turn the heat back up, and cook for about 4 minutes. The glass bowls will sound like they are doing a little tap dance. The whites should be set and the yolks still runny.

5. Turn off the heat, and carefully remove the hot bowls from the pan with a slotted spoon, spatula, or tongs. Serve with slices of hot buttered toast.

For a meat and cheese version, add to each serving:

1 spoonful finely chopped cooked ham or bacon

1 small spoonful finely chopped chives or scallions, greens thinly sliced

Salt and freshly ground black pepper

1 small spoonful grated cheddar cheese or other cheese of your choice

PROCEDURE
1. Mix together the ham or bacon and chives or scallions.
2. Place half in the buttered bowl.
3. Add the cream and break the egg on top.
4. Sprinkle the remaining ham or bacon and chives, a little salt and pepper, and cheese on top.
5. Cook as above.

Note If you use a real coddler like my mom's, it may take double the time for the egg to cook since the porcelain will need to heat up.

Baked Up Bacon

This is a foolproof way to cook up bacon. Instead of cooking in a pan on the stovetop where greasy spatters can be the rule, I bake it in the oven while I continue making the rest of breakfast, lunch, or supper. If you line your sheet pan with foil, cleanup is a snap. Bake extra slices for adding to sandwiches, baked potatoes, or for sprinkling on top of soups and salads.

MAKES 3 TO 4 SERVINGS

INGREDIENTS   8 slices bacon

PROCEDURE
1. Preheat oven to 375°F (190°C).
2. Cover a sheet pan with foil. If you don't have a sheet pan, use a skillet with or without the foil.
3. Lay the slices of bacon on top of the foil, or directly on the pan. Bake for 20 to 25 minutes until the fat is mostly rendered out and the edges of the bacon are brown and crispy.
4. Drain on paper towels and serve.

Note I use thickly sliced bacon. If you are using thinly sliced bacon, it will take less time to bake.

One-Bowl Oats with Egg, Avocado, and Salsa

When I first asked for an egg to top my bowl of oats at a breakfast buffet, the cook looked in amazement as I then topped it off with slices of avocado, a spoonful of chopped red onions, and a liberal dousing of hot sauce. When I returned the next time and made the same request, he smiled and told me that he had tried my combination and was now a convert.

MAKES 1 BOWL

INGREDIENTS

1 cup (236 ml) water

½ cup (70 g) whole rolled oats

Pinch of salt

1 to 2 large eggs

¼ avocado, sliced

Chopped red onion

Salsa or hot sauce

Salt and freshly ground black pepper

PROCEDURE

1. Place water, oats, and salt in a small saucepan. Bring to a boil. Lower heat and simmer for about 5 minutes until the oats have absorbed the water. Place in an individual serving bowl.
2. Cook up eggs however you like and place on top of the oats.
3. Add avocado slices, onion, and salsa or hot sauce.
4. Season with salt and pepper to taste.

An Easy Way to Cook Perfect Eggs

When cooking eggs in the frying pan, I find it frustrating that the bottoms get cooked before the tops are done, or that sometimes the yolks break when I flip them over. Many years ago on a road trip, I stopped in for breakfast at a small rural café and ordered eggs cooked medium. I watched as the cook cracked my eggs into a hot greased pan, and after a minute added a little hot water, and placed a cover on top. When the cover came off, there were two perfectly cooked eggs—not too runny, not too hard, but with just the right amount of yellow yolk ooze. You may already know about cooking eggs this way, but it was new to me. Since then, I've shared this easy technique with many who have enjoyed what they call "perfect eggs" at my table.

Easy No-Cook Chilly Oats

I love hot cooked oatmeal and, since I don't want to relegate my breakfast oats to the shelf during the summer, I eat them uncooked. I can promise you that this is one of the easiest, quickest, and tastiest breakfasts ever. If you aren't fond of raw oats, summer or not, simply cook them up as in One-Bowl Oats with Egg, Avocado, and Salsa (see page 26) and add the other ingredients listed here. Either way, oats are a great way to start the day.

MAKES 1 BOWL

INGREDIENTS

Plain yogurt

Whole rolled oats, uncooked

Walnuts, pecans, or other nuts of your choice

Frozen or fresh fruit, cut into bite-size pieces

Pure grade A or B maple syrup

Hulled hemp seed hearts or other toppings you like (optional)

PROCEDURE

1. Put a few soup spoonfuls of yogurt in a bowl.
2. Sprinkle on top a handful of oats, some nuts, fruit, and finish off with a drizzle of maple syrup.
3. Add an optional sprinkling of hemp hearts or other toppings of your choice.

My First Cookbooks

My first cookbook, *Betty Crocker's Cookbook for Boys and Girls*, was a gift from my mom when I was six years old. I spent hours poring over the photos and recipes, with names like Chili Concoction, Eggs in a Frame, and Three Men in a Boat. I was so proud the first time I made a meal all by myself, with a little knife supervision from Mom, of course. Those were the days when grocery stores and gas stations gave out green and blue chip stamps. My brother and I filled stamp books, dreaming about what we would choose to "buy" with them from the catalog. Mom was always fair about giving us turns to pick, and when it was mine I chose what I considered to be my first grown-up cookbook—the red-and-white–checkered *Better Homes and Gardens Cook Book*. I still have both cookbooks, along with the copy of *The Joy of Cooking* she gave to me on my eighteenth birthday. Both my mom and grandmother called that one "Rombauer" after the author, and I do, too. My copy of Rombauer sits on the shelf right next to my mom's World War II edition. *The Fannie Farmer Cookbook* joined the lineup in my mid-20s when I first married.

Greg's Granola

Granola has been on my breakfast table since the 1960s when we had to make our own. It's all grown up now and gone mainstream with many great options to choose from at the store, but I still like to make it. One of my favorites is this version by Chef Greg Atkinson, who lives on Bainbridge Island. Greg says the keys to success are using real maple syrup and having good, sturdy baking sheets. I like to serve it in bowls topped with yogurt, berries, or slices from a perfectly ripe peach. This recipe makes about 5 cups and can easily be doubled.

MAKES 10 (½-CUP) SERVINGS

INGREDIENTS

4 cups (560 g) whole rolled oats

½ cup (120 ml) vegetable oil

½ cup (120 ml) honey

½ cup (120 ml) grade A or B maple syrup

2 tablespoons (30 ml) water

1½ teaspoons vanilla extract

1½ teaspoons kosher salt

PROCEDURE

1. Preheat oven to 325°F (160°C). Pile the oats into a large mixing bowl.
2. In a saucepan over medium-high heat, combine oil, honey, maple syrup, water, vanilla extract, and salt. Bring the mixture to a boil, stirring to prevent it from boiling over. Pour the syrup over the oats and stir until the mixture is well combined.
3. Spread the granola onto a cookie sheet and bake in the preheated oven for 20 minutes. Stir the granola, but don't break up the clumps entirely.
4. Return the granola to the oven and turn it off. Allow the granola to cool in the oven. This ensures that the cereal will be dry enough to keep. Transfer the cooled granola to an airtight container. Properly dried and cooled before it's packed, homemade granola can stay fresh for two weeks and frozen for up to three months.

Note This can also be made in a slow cooker. Set on low, and stir every 15 minutes or so. Then spread on a sheet pan as above to finish drying out.

Dutch Baked Baby

You might think of this dish as a giant popover. Even on a busy morning, it's quite easy to make. I bake the baby in a well-seasoned 10-inch cast-iron fry pan that my mom gave to me forty years ago. This recipe can also be made with gluten-free flour, almond milk, and a non-dairy butter substitute.

MAKES 2 TO 3 SERVINGS

DOUGH

2 tablespoons (30 ml) melted butter, plus more for greasing the pan

½ cup (73 g) unbleached all-purpose flour

½ teaspoon salt

3 large eggs

½ cup (125 ml) milk

TOPPINGS

Powdered sugar

Lemon juice

Grade A or B maple syrup

Butter

Jam

PROCEDURE

1. Preheat the oven to 450°F (230°C). Butter the bottom and sides of a large cast-iron or other heavy frying pan and set aside.
2. Sift the flour with salt and set aside.
3. Crack the eggs into a medium-size bowl and fork beat until well blended.
4. Add the sifted flour to the eggs two tablespoons at a time, fork beating after each addition until smooth.
5. Add the milk in two additions, mixing lightly with the fork after each.
6. Add the 2 tablespoons melted butter, and mix lightly once again.
7. Pour the batter into the greased frying pan. Bake in the preheated oven for 25 minutes. It will poof up.
8. Sprinkle with powdered sugar and an optional squeeze of lemon juice, or serve with warm maple syrup and butter, or jam of choice on top or on the side.
9. Cut pieces with knife or pie server.

Sunday Brunch Banana Pancakes

In every home in which I have lived since my early twenties, I have made these pancakes. My mom and grandmother loved them, my kids loved them, and so have friends, boyfriends, and wuzbands. A couple of hints before you start: You'll need two medium-size bowls—one for the wet ingredients, one for the dry—plus a little bowl in which to mash the ripe bananas. To keep the already cooked pancakes warm until you are ready to serve, preheat your oven to 200°F (about 95°C), and set the serving platter on a rack inside. Place the first batch of cooked pancakes onto the platter, and add to it as you bake each successive batch. When you've used up all the batter and the pancakes are cooked, put on your oven mitts, remove the platter from the oven, and set it on top of a hot pad at the table. Then take off your apron, join the table, and enjoy breakfast.

SERVES 6

INGREDIENTS

2 cups (500 ml) milk

¼ cup (60 ml) butter, melted, or safflower oil

2 large eggs

2 cups (292 g) unbleached all-purpose flour

2 teaspoons aluminum-free baking powder

¼ cup (50 g) granulated sugar

1 teaspoon salt

1 to 2 ripe bananas, mashed

Extra butter or oil for cooking

TOPPING

Grade A or B maple syrup

Butter

CONTINUED

PROCEDURE
1. Add the milk, butter or oil, and eggs into a medium-size mixing bowl, and fork beat or whisk lightly.
2. In another medium-size bowl, mix together the flour, baking powder, sugar, and salt.
3. In a small bowl, mash the bananas with a fork.
4. Add the flour to the egg-and-milk mixture, and stir lightly just until the flour looks damp. Don't overmix.
5. Add the banana and stir lightly to mix.
6. Set an ovenproof platter or dish inside the oven and preheat the oven to 200°F (about 95°C) to keep the pancakes warm.
7. Set a griddle or frying pan over medium heat, and melt a pat of butter or heat some oil in the pan. You'll know if the pan is ready if you sprinkle a few drops of cold water onto the hot pan and they sizzle and dance around.
8. Take ¼ cup of batter and pour it onto the hot pan or griddle. Quickly fill the pan with additional ¼ cups of batter, leaving some space between each addition.
9. Bake on the griddle until the top of the pancake is full of bubbles. Don't be tempted to turn the pancake until you see them. Flip the pancake with a spatula and cook the other side until golden. It's okay to lift it up a bit to take a peek. Place the cooked pancakes in the warm oven.
10. Add more butter or oil to the pan, add more pancake batter and cook as before.
11. When all are cooked, remove from oven, and serve with maple syrup and butter.

How to Tell if Baking Powder Is Fresh

Baking powder doesn't last forever, so if you haven't used it for a while, do this simple test to make sure it is still active. In a small bowl, place 1 teaspoon baking powder. Pour over ½ cup (120 ml) of boiling water. If you see vigorous bubbling, it's active. If you see none or just a few bubbles, toss it out and head to the store for a new can of aluminum-free baking powder. With a sharpie, mark on the lid the date you opened it.

Stuffed French Toast

Duncan made the shift to attending the local high school after being homeschooled, so when he wasn't catching the big yellow bus, I switched hats and became the mom taxi before starting my own workday. On those early mornings, I made a lot of French toast. This version, with a delicious soft cheese filling, definitely fills the belly of growing teenagers with voracious appetites. Once you've done this recipe a few times, you'll find it takes about 10 minutes from fridge to plate for the stuffed version, and 5 if unstuffed.

SERVES 4

FRENCH TOAST

2 large eggs

¾ cup (185 ml) milk

A pinch of salt

2 tablespoons granulated sugar or grade A or B maple syrup

1 teaspoon vanilla extract

¼ to ½ teaspoon cinnamon

8 slices bread (2 for each serving)

FILLING

8 ounces (225 g) goat cheese, cream cheese, or ricotta cheese

1 tablespoon grade A or B maple syrup

½ teaspoon vanilla extract

TOPPING

Butter

Grade A or B maple syrup

1. Fork beat the eggs. Add the milk, salt, sugar, vanilla, and cinnamon, and mix again until well blended. Pour into a large casserole dish.
2. For the filling, place the cheese in a stand mixer or a bowl if using a hand-beater. Mix gradually, increasing the speed so that the cheese is softer (especially in the case of the goat or cream cheese). Add the maple syrup and vanilla and mix well again. Set aside.
3. Place two pieces of bread into the egg mixture. Let sit for thirty seconds or so, and then turn over to coat the other side. Repeat with additional bread slices. While the pieces of bread are soaking, melt butter in a wide skillet. Mine is 12 inches (30 cm) wide, so I can place four slices in at once.
4. Place the soaked bread in the skillet and cook over medium heat until the bottom of the bread is a golden brown. Flip over both slices of bread.
5. While the second side is cooking in the skillet, spread the cheese mixture on top of half the slices. For example, if you have four slices in the pan, you will cover only two with the spread.
6. When the bottom of the slices are golden brown, take a spatula, and carefully lift each cheese-topped slice onto a plate. Place the second piece on top to stuff the French toast.
7. Serve with butter and maple syrup.

With Fresh Fruit

Sauté peach or other fruit slices in butter. Place between two layers of bread for a stuffed fruit variation or place the fruit on top of one slice for an open-face version.

With Jam

Spread with your favorite jam and sprinkle on some nuts.

Savory

For a sweet and savory version, crumble up crisp bacon or slices of sausage and place between the cooked slices with or without the filling. Syrup is optional.

Unstuffed

For plain French toast, leave the filling out completely.

A Strong Intuition

We were deep into the building of our post-and-beam home; walls were up, roof was finished, sub-flooring was down with insulation underneath, and the rough plumbing was in. On a Saturday afternoon, Duncan and his dad headed into town to go to the grocery store and do a few other errands. I stayed home to stoke the wood stove, stir the soup, and read a book, but after a while I had a funny feeling that I needed to go up the hill to check on our new house. I put on my coat and shoes, and headed out the door. As I started up the hill, I heard a rushing and whooshing noise. The closer I got, the louder it got. I opened the sliding doors and saw 3 to 4 inches of water covering the entire floor. I had no idea where the turn-off valve to the well was and was petrified that much of our hard work would have to be re-done.

I went back outside and sent out a silent message as strongly as I could that I needed my boys to drop everything and come back home right away. Like a radio beacon, I kept putting out the message, "Come Home Now. Come Home Now." About 10 minutes later, I heard the sound of our truck coming up the drive. I cried out, "The house is flooding!" My husband and son got right out of the car and we all ran up the hill. The water valve into the house had failed. My husband turned off the water and then cut a few holes in the new sub-flooring to let the water drain. After we all calmed down, he told me that he had gotten a very strong intuition that he needed to come home right away. Even though he had a grocery cart full of supplies, he left it in the aisle, walked out of the store, got into the truck with our son, and they headed home.

The next day, he installed a stronger valve and showed me where and how to turn off the water so this little drama would never happen again. The floor and insulation over time dried out and were saved, and none of us ever doubted that the power of intuition had a great deal to do with it all.

Maple Almond Surprise Muffins

A family favorite with an almond batter surprise tucked inside. Be sure to grease the top of the muffin tin, too.

MAKES 12 MUFFINS

INGREDIENTS

Butter or oil, to grease the muffin tins

¼ cup (60 ml) melted butter

2¼ cups (328 g) unbleached all-purpose flour, or 2¼ cups (355 g) gluten-free flour

2 teaspoons aluminum-free baking powder

¼ teaspoon salt

1¼ cups (125 ml) milk

¼ cup (60 ml) grade A or B maple syrup

½ teaspoon vanilla extract or other flavor extract

1 large egg, beaten

1 pinch of freshly ground nutmeg

FILLING

½ cup (120 ml) grade A or B maple syrup

½ cup (55 g) finely chopped almonds

6 tablespoons (54 g) unbleached all-purpose flour

2 tablespoons (30 ml) melted butter

PROCEDURE

1. Preheat oven to 400°F (200°C) and grease a muffin tin with butter or oil.
2. Melt butter and set aside.
3. In a medium-size bowl, mix together the flour, baking powder, and salt.
4. In another medium-size bowl, mix together the milk, melted butter, maple syrup, vanilla extract, egg, and nutmeg.
5. In a third medium-size bowl, mix together the maple syrup, almonds, flour, and melted butter for the filling and set aside.
6. Combine the dry mixture and wet mixture in one bowl and stir until just moist.
7. Spoon into a greased muffin tin in three layers: 1 tablespoon muffin batter, 1 tablespoon almond mixture, 1 tablespoon muffin batter.
8. Bake in the preheated oven for 20 minutes.

Berry Good Coffee Cake, page 42

Berry Good Coffee Cake

Blackberries abound in alleyways and roadsides on Washington's Olympic Peninsula. During the late summer, you will see pickers with purple-stained fingers along byways filling buckets and boxes with dark ripe fruit. It's a tasty outing because you sample the berries as you pick. Blackberries freeze beautifully, too. This coffee cake is a wonderful way to enjoy the taste of summer all year long. One little tip from this longtime berry picker—blackberries have thorns, so be sure to wear a long-sleeve shirt and one that you won't mind getting stained.

MAKES 6 TO 8 SERVINGS

INGREDIENTS

Butter and flour or parchment paper for greasing baking dish

1 cup (about 144 g) blackberries or other berries of your choice

¾ cup (150 g) plus 1⅓ cups (233 g) granulated sugar

2½ cups (363 g) unbleached all-purpose flour

2 teaspoons aluminum-free baking powder

½ teaspoon baking soda

¼ teaspoon salt

¾ cup (175 g) butter, softened

4 large eggs

1½ teaspoons vanilla extract

1½ cups (368 g) sour cream or plain yogurt

GLAZE

2 tablespoons (30 ml) heavy cream or half and half

1 cup (100 g) powdered sugar

½ teaspoon vanilla extract

1. Preheat oven to 350°F (180°C). Butter an 8-inch (20-cm) square baking dish and dust with flour, or line with a sheet of parchment paper.
2. Mix the blackberries and ¾ cup sugar together, and set aside.
3. In a medium-size bowl, combine flour, baking powder, baking soda, and salt, and mix well with a fork or whisk.
4. In another medium-size bowl, cream the butter and ⅓ cup sugar for about 3 minutes until light and fluffy. I use an electric hand beater.
5. Add the eggs one at a time into the creamed mixture, and mix lightly after each addition. Add the vanilla and mix again.
6. Stir in the sour cream or yogurt.
7. Add the dry ingredients and stir gently until just mixed.
8. Pour half the batter into the greased and floured cake pan.
9. Top evenly with the blackberry mixture.
10. Pour the remaining batter evenly over the top.
11. Bake in preheated oven for 50 minutes or until a toothpick inserted into the center of the coffee cake comes out clean with no streaks of batter. A few small crumbs are okay. The coffee cake may puff up a bit above the rim of the pan. Remove from oven and let cool.
12. Combine the cream, sugar, and vanilla for the glaze and drizzle on top.

Note This can also be made in a buttered and floured angel food tube cake pan. Pour a third of the batter into the tube cake pan, followed by half of the berry mixture. Repeat and top with the last third of the batter. Once cooled, run a sharp knife around the edge of the coffee cake, give it a sharp rap on the counter, invert it onto a serving plate, and drizzle with the glaze.

Pie Cottage Scones

Fresh-baked scones are wonderful for breakfast, elevenses, and any time you need a little pick-me-up with a spot of tea or cup of cocoa. Don't worry about being too exact with the ingredients. If you are off a bit here or there, it's okay. The recipe seems to work out fine every time.

MAKES 12 TO 16 SCONES

INGREDIENTS

4 cups (548 g) unbleached all-purpose flour or gluten-free flour mix

½ cup (100 g) granulated sugar

⅛ teaspoon baking soda

Pinch of salt

1½ tablespoons aluminum-free baking powder

1 tablespoon poppy seeds, or zest of one orange or lemon (optional)

1 large egg

1¼ cups (280 g) sour cream or plain yogurt

½ cup (115 ml) melted butter or safflower oil

1 cup (240 ml) heavy cream, half and half, milk, or even milk mixed with some yogurt

½ to 1 teaspoon flavor extract of your choice (vanilla, almond, or orange)

2 teaspoons milk or half and half, for brushing

2 to 3 teaspoons granulated sugar, for sprinkling

PROCEDURE

1. Preheat oven to 425°F (220°C).
2. In a large bowl, mix all the dry ingredients with a fork including the optional poppy seeds or citrus zest.
3. Make a well on top of the flour mixture and crack the egg on top. Add the sour cream and all the other liquid ingredients including flavor extract. With a fork, mix together quickly until everything has just come together but not as well mixed as cookie dough.
4. On a floured surface, form into two balls and pat each to the size of your hand. With a brush, paint on some milk, and sprinkle with sugar.
5. Cut each round into 6 or 8 wedges and place on a parchment-covered or lightly greased baking sheet.
6. Bake in preheated oven for 15 to 20 minutes. They should look golden brown on top and the kitchen will smell really good. Serve with jam and butter.

Cobb Salad, page 76

High Noon

Chapter Two

"When it was time to eat, we ran down to the water to wash the sand off so it wouldn't get into our sandwiches."

A Picnic Basket Full

When I was a little girl, summertime and weekends were for family picnics. My grandmother and mom would load toys, blanket, a lunch-filled picnic basket, and me and my big brother into our big-finned, baby blue Plymouth station wagon, and we set off for a day at the beach. My grandmother wore a big sunhat on her head but neither my brother nor I ever did. When our noses and shoulders got too red, they were painted white with the zinc oxide packed in my mom's purse.

While my mom and grandmother kept watch, the two of us waded and splashed in the water. My brother, who was four years older and taller than me, could wade out farther. I wanted to join him but was told that if my feet started to float off the sand, I had to come back. We built sand castles, and buried each other in the sand. When it was time to eat, we ran down to the water to wash the sand off so it wouldn't get into our sandwiches.

Our lunch was packed in a big wicker picnic hamper. It had a set of multicolor melmac dishes and cups, green napkins, and strong fabric ribbons, secured on the underside of the cover that held silverware in neat rows. There was plenty of room for sandwiches, potato salad, slaw, cookies, and the red Hawaiian punch that everyone served when we were kids. Not realizing what a treasure it was, I let the picnic hamper go in a garage sale after Mom passed away, along with lots of things that were stored in the garage. I didn't let go of my treasure trove of memories, some of which were the meals shared from that picnic basket, with many of these easy lunchtime recipes that I still make today.

Make-Ahead Layered Salad, page 66

Nut Butter Sandwich Reimagined Ten Ways

I ate lots of peanut butter sandwiches when I was growing up. They were easy to pack for picnics and, at least once a week if not more, my mom sent me off to school with one in my lunch pail. First she spread a layer of butter on a slice of white bread, another layer of sugar-laced peanut butter, which was what was available in the 1950s, and topped it off with a final layer of grape jelly. As a grown-up, I began to play around with different ingredients to change up the PB&J of my youth. Here are a few ideas to whet your appetite. Mix and match until you find the perfect combination. Nut butter sandwiches are good grilled, too. Just spread softened butter on the outside of both slices of bread and grill until golden brown. Any nut butter may be substituted for peanut butter.

MAKES 1 SANDWICH

With Peppers and Arugula

2 slices of your favorite bread

Butter (optional)

Peanut butter, preferably one that is not sweetened with sugar

Marinated red peppers or other peppers of your choice—the amount is up to you

Salt

Arugula

With Bacon

2 slices of your favorite bread

Butter (optional)

Peanut butter, preferably one that is not sweetened with sugar

Several slices of bacon, cooked

Arugula or spinach (optional)

Several slices of apple (optional)

With Pickles

2 slices of your favorite bread

Butter (optional)

Peanut butter, preferably one that is not sweetened with sugar

Dill or bread-and-butter pickles

Sharp cheddar cheese (optional)

With Banana

2 slices of your favorite bread

Butter (optional)

Banana, sliced

Peanut butter, preferably one that is not sweetened with sugar

Nutella (optional)

With Veggies and Hot Sauce

2 slices of your favorite bread

Butter (optional)

Peanut butter, preferably one that is not sweetened with sugar

Sliced cucumbers

Shredded carrots

Chopped red onions

Arugula or spinach

Hot sauce of your choice

With Granola and Jam

2 slices of your favorite bread

Butter (optional)

Peanut butter, preferably one that is not sweetened with sugar

Crunchy granola

Your favorite jam

CONTINUED

With Chips

2 slices of your favorite bread

Butter (optional)

Peanut butter, preferably one that is not sweetened with sugar

Chips of your choice: potato, tortilla, or vegetable

With Berries

2 slices of your favorite bread

Butter (optional)

Peanut butter, preferably one that is not sweetened with sugar

A small handful of ripe berries (blueberries and raspberries are nice)

With Egg

2 slices of your favorite bread

Butter (optional)

Peanut butter, preferably one that is not sweetened with sugar

1 large poached or fried egg

With Honey

2 slices of your favorite bread

Butter (optional)

Peanut butter, preferably one that is not sweetened with sugar

Honey

Kitchen Sink Nachos with Peppers, Beans, and Cheese

I never tire of eating nachos. They're quick to make and nice to share with friends anytime of the day or to enjoy all by myself when I'm watching a movie on my laptop. I use homemade refried or seasoned black beans if I have them already made, and if not, my trusty can opener is called into service to open a can of black beans.

SERVES 4 TO 6

INGREDIENTS

1 bag salted or unsalted corn tortilla chips

1 pound (454 g) jack or jalapeño jack cheese, grated

One 15.25-ounce (432-g) can black beans, drained, or homemade refried beans (recipe follows)

One 2.25-ounce (64-g) can sliced ripe black olives

TOPPING

1 avocado, sliced

1 tomato, diced

4 to 5 scallions, whites and greens, thinly sliced

Sour cream

Lettuce, grated or torn

Salsa

Tasty Guacamole (see page 59)

PROCEDURE

1. Preheat oven to 400°F (200°C).
2. Cover a cookie sheet with half of the tortilla chips.
3. Sprinkle one third of the cheese on top of the chips.
4. Spoon half the beans evenly over the cheese.
5. Spoon half of the olives evenly over the beans.
6. Bake in preheated oven for 4 minutes.
7. Remove from oven and quickly add the second layer of chips, cheese, beans, and one final layer of cheese. Bake for another 4 minutes until cheese is bubbly.
8. Top with avocado, tomato, scallions, sour cream, lettuce, salsa, and guacamole.

How to Cook a Pot of Pinto Beans for Refried Beans

Have you heard the words, *Don't bother the pot*? They are exactly the ones you want to think of when you are cooking up a pot of pinto beans. Once the beans start to cook, you don't need to stir, or do much of anything except check on them now and then to make sure they have enough water. My family likes the flavor of lard in these beans, but you can use canola or safflower oil, too. Some say that the flavor of beans is better on the second day, and I completely agree. Once they are cooled, use them as they are, or smoosh them with a potato masher for refried beans to use in Black Bean and Meat of Your Choice Enchiladas (see page 228), Duncan's Fish Tacos (see page 231), or Quick Quesadillas (see page 56). They can also be frozen for about six months in 2-cup containers, and defrosted as needed.

MAKES ABOUT 3 CUPS

INGREDIENTS

½ pound (225 g) pinto beans

6 cups (1.4 l) water to cover them

1 tablespoon lard or canola oil

½ small onion, chopped

1½ teaspoons salt

¼ cup (60 g) lard or canola oil, to make the refried beans

PROCEDURE

1. Rinse the beans well, and pick out any little stones or pebbles you might see.
2. Put the beans in the pot, and cover with water.
3. Add the lard or oil, and onion.
4. Bring to a boil. Cover the pot, turn down the heat, and simmer for an hour and a half until the beans are soft.
5. Add the salt and simmer for 30 minutes longer. The beans will get softer.
6. Let them cool, then place in the refrigerator overnight.
7. Smoosh the cooled, cooked beans and liquid with a potato masher, or pulse in a food processor until roughly pureed.
8. Heat ¼ cup (60 g) lard or oil in a cast-iron frying pan over medium-high heat.
9. Add the smooshed beans, and cook as you stir and scrape the bottom of the pan. It's okay if they get crusty. Fold that part back into the more moist part—just don't let the beans burn.
10. When the beans are looking thick, remove from the heat. You can use now, or cool and freeze for later.

Quick Quesadillas

You can add just about anything to the inside of a quesadilla, including last night's leftovers. Very quick to fix, able to satisfy hungry toddlers and growing teenagers while quelling the occasional hunger tantrums on both ends of that spectrum, quesadillas are a perfect nosh—for an empty nester, too.

MAKES 4

INGREDIENTS

One 15.25-ounce (432-g) can black beans, drained, or homemade refried beans (see page 55)

1½ cups (170 g) grated cheddar or jack cheese or a mix

Leftovers you have in the fridge (optional)

8 flour tortillas

Butter

TOPPING

Avocado slices

Red onion, chopped small

Cilantro, chopped

Tasty Guacamole (see page 59), for serving

Hot sauce or salsa, for serving

Lime wedges, for serving

PROCEDURE

1. Evenly spread some beans, cheese, and optional leftovers on half of the tortillas. Cover with remaining tortillas.
2. Heat a cast-iron pan or griddle over medium heat. Add butter and let melt.
3. Place one or more quesadillas on the heated pan or griddle and cook until the cheese begins to melt and the underside is light brown. With a spatula, carefully flip each quesadilla over and continue cooking until the underside is light brown.
4. Remove to a cutting board and cut into wedges using a pizza cutter or knife.
5. Top with a few pieces of avocado, red onion, and cilantro, and serve with guacamole, hot sauce or salsa, and lime wedges to squeeze over the top.

Note I have also made these with large gluten-free rice tortillas.

Tasty Guacamole

When I was first married in my mid-twenties, I lived in a carriage house at the foot of the Santa Barbara Riviera. The kitchen window was so close to the branch of an avocado tree that I could reach my hand out and pick off the ripe fruits. Technically, the tree was in the neighbor's yard, but I claimed that one branch as mine. When the round softball-size fruits dropped from the higher branches, there was a serious thud on the roof, which was the signal to make guacamole. The avocados on that tree were so big that it only took one.

SERVES 4

INGREDIENTS
3 ripe medium-size avocados (or one big avocado picked right out the kitchen window)

Fresh squeezed juice of ½ lemon or lime

⅓ teaspoon salt

¼ cup (65 ml) favorite salsa, mild, medium, or hot

PROCEDURE

1. Cut the avocados in half and remove the pits. Scoop out the flesh from two of the avocados, place in a medium-size bowl, and smoosh with a fork.

2. With a knife, carefully score the flesh of half of the remaining avocado into ½- to ¾-inch (1- to 2-cm) size pieces. Scoop out the pieces with a spoon and place on top of the smooshed avocado already in the bowl. Repeat with the remaining half.

3. Squeeze the lemon or lime juice into the bowl. Add salt and salsa, and lightly mix together with a fork. Add more salt, lemon, or lime to your own taste.

4. Serve with Quick Quesadillas (see page 56), Black Bean and Meat of Your Choice Enchiladas (see page 228), Veggie Mex Casserole (see page 224), or a big bowl of tortilla chips.

Note Place avocado pits in leftover guacamole to help keep it from turning brown.

Almost Hummus

I was preparing some hummus to take on a weekend campout with long-time girl-friends and found that I didn't have any tahini with which it is traditionally made. I decided to make a batch without, and took it along with me hoping for the best. I set it out on the table with some chips. A meal seasoned with fresh air and the camaraderie of good friends always tastes better to me, and maybe that was what made this hummus taste so good. At the end of the weekend, many asked for the recipe. Since then, I've continued to make it the same way and haven't missed the tahini at all. The carrot gives a slightly sweet flavor to the beans, and the recipe freezes beautifully.

MAKES ABOUT 2½ CUPS (615 G)

INGREDIENTS

1 cup (200 g) dry garbanzo beans

1 tablespoon (15 ml) olive oil

1½ medium onions, finely chopped

1 medium carrot, peeled and diced

3 cloves garlic, minced

1 tablespoon (15 ml) tamari

3 tablespoons (45 ml) fresh squeezed lemon juice

1 teaspoon ground cumin

⅛ to ¼ teaspoon cayenne pepper (optional)

¼ teaspoon salt

PROCEDURE

1. Place dry, uncooked garbanzo beans in a large pot, and cover with water. Let them sit overnight.

2. Bring to a boil and simmer uncovered until tender, about 2 to 3 hours. Add water as needed. Remove from heat, drain, and buzz up in a food processor until smooth, or mash well with a potato masher.

3. Heat oil in a skillet and sauté the onions, carrot, and garlic until tender and the onions are golden brown.

4. Add the sautéed vegetables, tamari, lemon juice, cumin, cayenne (if using), and salt, and buzz up once again. Taste and add more salt to your own taste.

Note If you would like to use tahini, add 1 cup to the mashed beans along with the sautéed vegetables and spices, and process thoroughly. I prefer to cook my own garbanzo beans for hummus, but if you are in a hurry, two 15.5-ounce cans (878 g total) garbanzo beans, drained and pureed, will work.

Black Bean Dip

I love black bean dip, and it makes a very quick lunch or appetizer to serve with chips and fresh-cut veggies. It's good in Quick Quesadillas, too (see page 56). I often double this recipe, and freeze the extra in yogurt containers. When I get close to reaching the bottom of one container, it's nice to have another on hand.

MAKES ABOUT 2 CUPS (400 G)

INGREDIENTS

1 cup (200 g) dry black beans, or one 15.5-ounce can (434 g total) black beans, drained

½ teaspoon salt, if using dry beans

1 tablespoon (15 ml) artisan apple cider vinegar

½ teaspoon onion powder

½ teaspoon garlic powder

½ teaspoon ground cumin

¼ teaspoon ground coriander

½ teaspoon dried oregano

¾ teaspoon salt, or more to taste

PROCEDURE

1. Skip this step if using canned beans. Rinse dry beans several times, place them in a Dutch oven or large-lidded pot, cover with water, and bring to a boil for 3 minutes. Remove and discard any foam on top. Let sit for 1 hour. Bring the beans back to a boil, turn the heat down, add salt, cover, and simmer for 60 to 90 minutes total until the beans are soft. Add extra water as needed. Older beans will take longer.

2. Drain beans. Add to food processor or blender with the remaining ingredients, and process until smooth. Add salt to taste and mix again.

Note A tablespoon or two of sour cream is a nice addition to the dip.

Fava Beans, Bread, and Pecorino

The wooden sign hanging outside of Ciro's bakery in Seattle read "Food and Philosophy." His bread was sturdy, rustic, and very tasty. It is the memory of an afternoon's conversation at his home that I count as an unexpected lesson in how to see.

We sat at a small table in his backyard, surrounded by his urban garden full of vegetables, fruit trees, flowers, and grape arbor. Ciro set a small mountain of homegrown fava beans, a wedge of Pecorino, a salty sheep's milk cheese that has been around since ancient Roman times, a bottle of his homemade red wine, two glasses, and some of his crusty bread on the table. He asked me to look at it all for a moment, and then motioned for me to tear a piece from the loaf while he filled our glasses. With a knife from his pocket, he sliced some cheese, and showed me how to open the jackets of the fava beans with my fingers.

We shared a bit of our life philosophies, and after the last sip of wine was taken, he waved his open hand, strong with years of kneading bread, across the table. "Look at the table now, Kate." The surface was covered with crumbs, empty fava jackets, and the last drops of wine in our glasses. The table was a record of our meal: our conversation, the love and sweet time that we had spent together doing what people have done for centuries—sharing time, food, and conversation with companions. "That's our history," he said. Since then, instead of seeing crumbs and spills, I see memories of words and time, well spent with family and friends.

Vegetable Pancakes

These savory pancakes are great for lunch, supper, or late-night snacks, and can be eaten hot or at room temperature. Each time I make them, they are slightly different, since whatever I have in my vegetable drawer is fair game to be added to the batter.

MAKES 4 TO 6 SERVINGS

INGREDIENTS

2 cups (292 g) unbleached all-purpose flour

1 large egg, fork beaten

2 tablespoons brown or granulated sugar

1 teaspoon salt

1½ cups milk (360 ml) (whole milk, half and half, or light coconut milk all work fine)

Water as needed

Suggestions for vegetables and meat to chop/shred/dice/slice:

Cabbage (any color or kind)

Carrot

Celery

Onion (red, white, or yellow)

Mung bean sprouts

Kale or other greens

Leftover meat or fish

Butter, oil, or lard to cook

Extra butter, for serving

Tamari, for serving

PROCEDURE

1. Mix the flour, egg, sugar, salt, and milk together in a large bowl until it looks like pancake batter. If it looks too thick, you can thin it out with a little water.
2. Shred, dice, or slice the vegetables. Chop or slice the leftover meat or fish. Fold everything into the batter.
3. Heat some oil, butter, or lard in a skillet or griddle, and cook on both sides until the pancakes are light brown on each side.
4. Serve with butter and tamari.

Make-Ahead Layered Salad

This retro salad can be made the night before, placed in the fridge, and pulled out for a picnic at the beach or a BBQ in the backyard with friends. Toss just before serving and be sure to light your vintage tiki torches, too.

SERVES 6

INGREDIENTS

1 small to medium head of iceberg lettuce

⅓ cup (100 g) scallions, whites and greens, thinly sliced

Several stalks of celery, thinly sliced in ¼-inch (5-mm) half moons

One 18-ounce (226-g) can sliced water chestnuts, drained

One 10-ounce (284-g) package frozen peas

2 cups (440 g) mayonnaise

2 tablespoons granulated sugar

1 teaspoon seasoning salt (such as Spike), or more to taste

¾ teaspoon garlic powder

1¼ cups (115 g) grated Parmigiano-Reggiano cheese

3 large hard-boiled eggs, crumbled

6 to 8 slices bacon, cooked crisp, drained on paper towels, and crumbled

PROCEDURE

1. Shred head of lettuce and place in a 9-by-13-inch (23-by-33-cm) baking pan or other dish of similar size.
2. On top of the lettuce, layer and spread evenly in this order: scallions, celery, water chestnuts, and frozen peas.
3. Spread the mayonnaise over the top sealing everything inside.
4. Sprinkle with sugar, seasoning salt, garlic powder, and cheese. Chill for 24 hours.
5. Just before serving, toss well, and top with crumbled eggs and bacon. You can also leave in layers, top with the eggs and bacon, and serve.

Stuffed Pita

Anything you can put in a sandwich, you can stuff into a pita. BLT? You bet. Tuna fish with slices of apples? Absolutely. Avocados, sprouts, and cheese? Always a classic. In the morning, I tuck in eggs and bacon with a bit of goat cheese and pesto, and head out to the deck with my coffee mug for a fresh-air breakfast. Last night's leftovers often find their way inside a pita, too. One of my favorites is this quick-to-make filling of sautéed vegetables seasoned with herbs, feta cheese, and olives.

SERVES 2 TO 4

INGREDIENTS

1 tablespoon (15 ml) olive oil

1 small head of broccoli, cut into small stem and flower pieces

1 small onion, chopped

3 cloves garlic, minced

½ teaspoon chopped fresh oregano leaves

A few leaves of fresh basil, chopped

1 small yellow or green zucchini squash, sliced

2 cups (144 g) mushrooms, sliced

⅓ cup (43 g) sliced black olives or other olives of your choice

⅓ teaspoon salt

Pinch of freshly ground black pepper

½ cup (75 g) feta cheese

2 whole pitas, cut in half

Spinach leaves

2 small tomatoes, sliced

PROCEDURE

1. In medium frying pan, heat olive oil over medium heat.
2. Add broccoli, onion, garlic, oregano, and basil and sauté for 2 to 3 minutes.
3. Add zucchini, mushrooms, olives, salt, and pepper and cook for 2 to 3 minutes more. Drain off extra juice. Stir in feta cheese.
4. Spoon the filling evenly into all four half pitas.
5. Tuck in some spinach leaves and slices of tomato in each pocket.

Teardrop Salad

Witnessing your child's heartbreak is hard no matter what their age. All you can do is hold them while they cry, and let them know that, as painful as it is now, they are one day closer to true happiness. I made this rice salad the day my son accepted his longtime sweetheart's choice to leave their relationship. The grains of rice remind me of his tears.

SERVES 6 TO 8

INGREDIENTS

3 cups (750 ml) water

1½ cups (270 g) white basmati rice (or other rice of your choice)

6 to 8 asparagus spears, or about ½ cup (65 g) fresh or frozen peas

3 scallions, whites and greens, thinly sliced

½ medium red pepper, diced

¼ cup chopped parsley

2 stalks celery, chopped small

½ teaspoon salt

¼ teaspoon freshly ground black pepper

¼ cup (60 ml) olive oil

Juice of ½ small lemon

½ cup (75 g) crumbled feta cheese

PROCEDURE

1. Bring water to a boil, add rice, and cook until done. For the white basmati, it takes about 20 minutes.
2. Steam asparagus spears in 1 inch (2.5 cm) of water for 4 minutes. Rinse in cold water. Chop in 1-inch (2.5-cm) pieces.
3. Add to the pot of rice the asparagus or peas, scallions, red pepper, parsley, and celery. Toss well to mix.
4. In a small bowl, mix salt, pepper, olive oil, and squeeze of half a lemon with a fork. Pour over rice and vegetables. Add crumbled feta cheese and toss again lightly.
5. Let sit for about 1 hour before serving.

Note White basmati rice cooks up very quickly. Brown basmati or white jasmine rice will take longer to cook.

Marinated Rice Salad with Tomato and Feta

The climate on the Olympic Peninsula is temperate enough that my little town of Port Angeles has a year-round farmers' market. During the summer, when the market is in full swing, it's easy to bring home crispy vegetables. This rice salad makes a nice canvas to feature their bright colors and fresh crunch. It's okay to improvise with other additions, such as carrots and radishes. This is a good salad to take on a picnic, too.

SERVES 6 TO 8

INGREDIENTS

1½ cups (300 g) uncooked white basmati rice

3 cups (750 ml) water

1 tablespoon (15 ml) safflower oil

¼ cup plus 1 tablespoon (65 ml) seasoned rice wine vinegar

4 scallions, whites and greens, thinly sliced

1 medium red, orange, yellow, or green pepper, chopped small

⅓ cup chopped parsley

2 stalks celery, sliced thin

One 8-ounce (226-g) can sliced water chestnuts, drained

¾ cup (90 g) peas, fresh or frozen

½ teaspoon salt

Freshly ground black pepper, to taste

⅓ cup (75 ml) olive oil

2 cups halved cherry tomatoes

1 cup (150 g) crumbled feta cheese

PROCEDURE

1. Rinse the rice and place in a medium-size pot. Cover with water. Bring to a boil. Lower heat to simmer and cover. Cook for 15 to 20 minutes, or until all the water is absorbed. Pour into a medium-size bowl and set aside to cool.
2. Sprinkle ¼ cup (50 ml) vinegar over the rice and mix.
3. Add the scallions, pepper, parsley, celery, water chestnuts, peas, salt, pepper, and olive oil, and toss well. Chill for about an hour.
4. Before serving, add one more tablespoon (15 ml) vinegar, tomato, and feta cheese, and toss again.

Summer Black Bean, Corn, and Pepper Salad

Black beans, yellow corn, and peppers of any color are so pretty when mixed together. They remind me of the swirling skirts my mom and I wore during Santa Barbara's Old Spanish Days when I was a little girl. One year, when our dresses matched, I remember her trying in vain to tame my curly hair so she could place a flower in it, just like hers.

SERVES 6

DRESSING

Juice of 1 lime

3 tablespoons (45 ml) citrus vinegar

2 tablespoons (30 ml) olive oil

1½ teaspoons cumin

¾ teaspoon salt

1 clove garlic, minced

SALAD

One 15-ounce (425-g) can black beans, rinsed and drained

One 15.5-ounce (439-g) can organic corn

1 medium red onion, chopped small

1 medium green or red pepper, seeded and chopped small

2 medium tomatoes, chopped

A handful cilantro, chopped

Salt and freshly ground black pepper

1 cup (150 g) crumbled feta cheese (optional)

1 head romaine lettuce

1 avocado, sliced

PROCEDURE

1. Make the dressing by mixing together the lime juice, vinegar, olive oil, cumin, salt, and garlic in a small bowl. Set aside.
2. In a large bowl, combine the beans, corn, onion, pepper, and the dressing. Toss well to mix.
3. Just before serving, add the tomatoes, cilantro, salt and pepper to taste, optional feta cheese, and toss again lightly.
4. Scoop some salad into each romaine leaf and set an avocado slice on top, or line a serving plate with all the leaves, scoop in the salad, and arrange the avocado slices on top.

Pear Salad with Stilton and Pecans

The most exotic cheeses we had when I was young were processed with pimentos, pre-grated parmesan in the round green cardboard container with the shaker top, or slices of American cheese. Based on my limited cheese palate, my mom was more than a little surprised when I ordered a blue cheese sandwich on pumpernickel bread one day at a restaurant. After the waitress took the order, Mom warned me that it would have a very strong flavor that she didn't think that I would like. Of course she was right, but as a moody teenager I was determined to prove her wrong. She could see that I was struggling with the flavor as I washed down each bite with plenty of ice water. Always the gentlewoman, she was polite enough not to say, "I told you so." Years later I was reintroduced to blue cheese in a salad. Served this way, it gave the salad star quality. Ripe Comice pears during the fall and winter are great for this salad, but apples work, too. In case you are wondering, I never ordered another blue cheese sandwich.

SERVES 4 TO 6

DRESSING

¼ cup (60 ml) good-quality balsamic vinegar, white wine vinegar, red wine vinegar, or rice wine vinegar

3 cloves garlic, minced or pressed

2 to 3 teaspoons Dijon mustard, depending on how strong you like it

½ teaspoon salt or seasoning salt (such as Spike)

⅛ teaspoon freshly ground black pepper

½ cup (60 ml) olive oil

SALAD

1 large or 2 small heads leaf lettuce, washed and torn into smaller pieces

1 to 2 ripe pears, cut into slices or bite-size chunks

½ cup (75 g) crumbled Stilton or other blue cheese

1 cup (100 g) walnuts or pecans, halved

PROCEDURE

1. Place vinegar, garlic, mustard, salt, pepper, and olive oil in a lidded jar. Shake well.
2. Put lettuce, pear, cheese, and walnuts or pecans in a medium-large bowl.
3. Shake dressing once again and drizzle some over the top.
4. Toss and serve.

Cobb Salad

As a young bride in my twenties, Mom took me out to lunch once a week. She loved hearing my updates about married life, fodder to share with her friends at their weekly beauty parlor appointments. I treasure those special hours we spent together as she passed away just a few short years later. Cobb Salad was always one of our favorites to share. Make the dressing a few hours before serving so the flavors can blend. Try Kerrygold's Cashel Blue Farmhouse Cheese or a ripe Stilton in this salad.

SERVES 4 TO 6

DRESSING

⅔ cup (150 ml) white wine vinegar

1 teaspoon Worcestershire sauce

1 clove garlic, peeled, minced or pressed

1 teaspoon granulated sugar

1 teaspoon dry mustard

1 teaspoon paprika

½ teaspoon freshly ground black pepper

1⅓ cups (325 ml) olive oil

SALAD

½ head iceberg lettuce, finely chopped

½ bunch watercress, finely chopped

1 small bunch endive, finely chopped

2 tablespoons minced chives

3 small tomatoes, peeled, seeded, and finely chopped

2 ½ cups (about 1 lb or 450 g) cooked boneless skinless chicken breast meat, chopped in bite-size pieces

6 slices bacon, cooked, drained, and crumbled

2 large hard-boiled eggs, diced

3 ounces (85 g) Stilton or other blue cheese, crumbled

1 to 2 ripe avocados, peeled and chopped into small pieces

PROCEDURE

1. Place the vinegar, Worcestershire sauce, garlic, sugar, mustard, paprika, pepper, and olive oil in a lidded jar. Shake well. Refrigerate for several hours.
2. Combine the vegetables, chicken, bacon, eggs, cheese, and avocado in a large bowl.
3. Shake the dressing and pour half over the salad. Toss lightly and add the remainder or serve on the side.

Sharing the Table with Marion

I read cookbooks like novels. My collection fills a double-size bookshelf, with overflow stacked on top and on the floor. I've cooked and baked my way through nearly all of them. With two or three new ones on my bedside table just waiting to be cracked open, I feel quite wealthy. My all-time favorite is my tattered copy of *The Fannie Farmer Cookbook*, written by Marion Cunningham. I received it as a newlywed in the late 1970s. I had cooked a lot before then, but these recipes, with their straightforward instructions and easy-to-find ingredients, gave me the confidence to try new dishes. It set a can-do standard for me. With *Fannie Farmer* propped up on my counter, I felt Marion with me in the kitchen, encouraging me to keep cooking and baking. Although my first marriage didn't last, my copy of her cookbook, now dog-eared, worn, and stained, did. I never dreamed that twenty-five years after first opening its cover, I would actually get to meet her in person.

Miss Cunningham and I were both attending a special dinner on a peach farm that was honoring Alice Waters and her Edible Schoolyard Project. The afternoon began with coolers in the packing shed, to be followed by a farm tour. The day was a real scorcher and too hot for Marion to join the tour—someone would need to stay behind to keep her company in the air-conditioned farm office. Laugh if you must,

but as a long-time resident of the Pacific Northwest, any day over sixty degrees is hot to me. I was more than happy to volunteer.

While other guests toured the orchards with sweet ripe peaches hanging from tree limbs, Marion and I were cool as cucumbers, sipping iced tea and chatting happily for over an hour about food, family, friends, and their importance in our lives. We agreed that the kitchen table is one of the most central places in a home, and that there is nothing that compares to the joy of family and friends gathered around it for even the simplest of meals. Fast food, eaten in the car while driving our kids to rehearsals, lessons, and sporting events, is just not the same as even five precious minutes around the table. I ventured to say that if ever I were to run for public office, my platform would include an "Eat Supper at Home Night" when, once a week, our entire nation would silence cell phones, computers, and TVs, in order to gather for one hour to share food and camaraderie. The art of conversation, which seems to be dying in favor of texting, would be practiced once again. I know it's a dream, but one which I will always hold dear.

Our hour passed quickly, and Marion and I were chatting it up like old friends, when our dinner mates returned from the orchard looking more than a little warm. When dinner was announced, arm in arm we headed out to the long candlelit table tucked in between two rows

of peach trees in the orchard, where it was now cooler. She motioned for me to take the seat just across from her so that we could continue to share the evening together and with others as they gathered at the table.

A few weeks later, when my new friend, Marion, travelled north to speak at an event just a few hours from my home, of course I went. Once again, I heard her thoughts about many of the ideas we had talked of during our unexpected one-on-one time on the peach farm. I carried my well-worn copy of *Fannie Farmer* with me in hopes that she would autograph it. She said that my copy might take the prize for being one of the most well used she had ever seen. "Well used and well loved," I said. A photo was snapped of the two of us while she was signing it, which I've tucked safely inside the cover. When I look at it, not only do I see the two of us standing there, but memories flood over me of first meals made as a newlywed, recipes shared at the table with a growing family, the sound of Marion's voice, and the sparkle in her eye as we talked of things that mattered to us, and maybe to you, too.

Salade Niçoise-ish

When I bought the little house that would one day turn into Pie Cottage, the deck out the back door was already wobbly. It was just a matter of time before it would need to be replaced. It hung on for fifteen years before my foot finally broke through the ricketey boards. I didn't have the money to replace it then, so avoided that spot by covering it with a small table. One year when friends came to house-sit, they moved the table and it nearly fell all the way through. It was very clear that the time had come for it to be replaced. I found a photo online of a much larger multi-level deck I really liked, and asked Duncan if he could build it for me. "Sure can, Mom," was his immediate reply. During the two weeks it took him to pour the new stout cement foundations and nail all-new boards on sturdy beams, I kept him well fed with quick meals that were easy to serve when he took breaks. This salad is one of them. You can add all the ingredients listed, or pick the ones you like best. The asparagus, green beans, and hard-boiled eggs can be cooked ahead and assembled just before serving. Pick a pretty platter and arrange the ingredients in a pleasing pattern on top of the lettuce leaves. If you are short on time, just put your chosen ingredients in a bowl, and toss with the dressing.

SERVES 4 TO 6

VINAIGRETTE

¼ cup (60 ml) good-quality balsamic vinegar, white wine vinegar, red wine vinegar, or rice wine vinegar

3 cloves garlic, peeled, minced or pressed

2 to 3 teaspoons Dijon mustard, depending on how strong you like it

½ teaspoon salt or seasoning salt (such as Spike)

⅛ teaspoon freshly ground black pepper

½ cup (120 ml) olive oil

1 pound (450 g) new red potatoes

1 pound (450 g) asparagus spears (optional)

½ teaspoon salt

1 pound (450 g) green beans, trimmed

1 head Bibb lettuce, center ribs removed

One 5-ounce (142-g) can oil-packed tuna, drained

½ each red and yellow bell peppers, cut into thin ¼-inch (5-mm) strips

2 medium tomatoes, quartered

12 radishes (optional)

¼ cup (60 g) capers, drained, rinsed, and patted dry

5 large hard-boiled eggs

½ red onion, sliced very thin

1 avocado, peeled and sliced (optional)

1 cup (115 g) Niçoise olives, pitted

Sprigs of parsley, for garnish

PROCEDURE

1. To make the vinaigrette, place the vinegar, garlic, mustard, salt, pepper, and olive oil in a lidded jar. Shake well and set aside.
2. Place potatoes in a lidded saucepan and cover with about 2 inches (5 cm) of water. Bring to a boil. Cover and lower the heat. Simmer for 15 minutes until the potatoes can be pierced easily with a fork but still hold their shape. Drain off the water.
3. Cut the warm potatoes into halves or quarters and place in a bowl. Pour half the vinaigrette over the potatoes, toss lightly, and set aside.
4. If using the asparagus, fill the saucepan halfway with water, turn the heat to high, and bring to a boil. Add the asparagus spears to the boiling water and cook for 2 to 3 minutes until tender but still firm to the bite. You don't want them to be mushy. Drain and rinse under cold water to stop the cooking.
5. Fill the saucepan halfway with water and add salt. Bring to a boil. Put the green beans in and boil for 3 to 4 minutes until just tender. Drain and rinse under cold water to stop the cooking.
6. Arrange a bed of lettuce on a serving platter. Drain and discard the oil from the tuna. Set aside.
7. Arrange the remaining ingredients in a pleasing pattern on the top of the lettuce.
8. Place the drained tuna in the center of the platter on top of lettuce.
9. Just before serving, drizzle the remaining vinaigrette over the top, or toss with the ingredients in a bowl.
10. Serve slightly warm or at room temperature.

Salade Niçoise-ish, page 80

Rice Noodle, Tofu, and Snow Pea Salad

This salad is perfect for gluten-free eaters since it uses rice noodles. Let the tofu marinate in the dressing for a few hours or overnight if possible.

SERVES 4 TO 6

INGREDIENTS

½ cup (115 ml) safflower oil

⅓ cup (75 ml) seasoned rice wine vinegar

2½ tablespoons (40 ml) tamari

14 ounces (397 g) firm or extra firm tofu, drained, patted dry, and cut in 1-inch (2.5-cm) cubes

2 tablespoons plus 1 teaspoon granulated sugar

3 tablespoons (45 ml) white wine vinegar

1½ teaspoons sesame oil

⅛ teaspoon crushed red pepper flakes

1 pound (450 g) package thin rice noodles

1 tablespoon (15 ml) peanut oil

1 teaspoon peeled and grated (or diced fine) fresh ginger

5 scallions, whites and greens, sliced on the diagonal into 1-inch (2.5-cm) pieces

1½ cups snow peas (240 g), stem and blossom ends cut off, sliced on the diagonal into 1-inch (2.5-cm) pieces

One 8-ounce (226-g) can sliced water chestnuts, drained

1 medium red pepper, sliced into thin strips (optional)

Extra rice wine vinegar

Note Be sure to use wheat-free tamari in the dressing if you are gluten-free.

---

1. In a medium bowl, mix together the oil, vinegar, and 1 tablesppoon tamari. Add the cubed tofu and mix gently. Cover and let marinate in the fridge overnight or at least a few hours.
2. In a small bowl, mix sugar, white wine vinegar, sesame oil, and red pepper flakes together. Set aside.
3. Bring water to boil in a medium saucepan. Turn off heat. Place rice noodles in a medium bowl and pour the water over them. Let them sit for 3 to 5 minutes, stirring occasionally, until they are soft. Drain, rinse briefly in a colander or large sieve strainer, and return to bowl.
4. Pour the vinegar-sesame oil dressing over noodles, toss, and set aside.
5. Pour the liquid off the tofu.
6. Heat peanut oil in a skillet or wok over medium heat, and sauté the tofu and ginger, until the tofu is slightly golden brown. Stand back when you put the marinated tofu in, as the oil will spatter and spit a bit. Have a towel handy to wipe up any on your stovetop.
7. Add the remaining 1½ tablespoons tamari, and stir lightly for about a minute.
8. Add the cooked tofu cubes, scallions, snow peas, water chestnuts, and optional red pepper to the noodles. Sprinkle a little extra rice wine vinegar over the top. Toss well and serve.

Miso Soup with Kimchi and Egg

No matter which side of the fence you are on in a divorce, it is never easy. Having the support of good friends, who can help to keep you centered when you are in the middle of one, is important. When my best friend Nancy called to find out how I was faring one day, I told her that I had lost my appetite and was rapidly losing weight. Now I didn't mind the weight loss so much, but we both knew that a stress-related divorce diet was not the way to accomplish it. I needed to eat. She asked me to look in the fridge to see what was there: miso, kimchi, and egg. As strange a combination as it may seem, these are three items that are usually in my fridge at any given time, and that day was no exception. She stayed on the phone with me, not only while I made this quick Asian-style soup with them, but also until I had finished every last bit of broth in the bowl. I can't say that this soup will heal a broken heart, but it kickstarted my appetite, and helped me through a very rough time.

SERVES 1

INGREDIENTS

2 cups (450 ml) water

1 to 2 tablespoons kimchi, roughly chopped

2 to 3 teaspoons (10 to 15 g) white miso paste

1 to 2 large eggs

1 scallion, greens thinly sliced

PROCEDURE

1. Place water in a small saucepan, turn up the heat, and bring to just below a boil.
2. Chop the kimchi and place in an individual serving bowl while you are waiting for the water.
3. Turn the heat to simmer, and whisk the miso paste into the water until dissolved.
4. Carefully break the eggs into the water, and simmer for 3 to 4 minutes. While they cook, take a slotted spoon and gently lift them an inch off the bottom of the saucepan to make sure they don't stick. Carefully remove the eggs, one at a time, with a slotted spoon, and place on top of the kimchi.
5. Pour the miso broth over the top of the eggs. Garnish with sliced scallion.

Pear Berry Pie, page 101

Short and Sweet Treats

Chapter Three

"Our noses and eyes told us when the cookies were ready."

Sadie's Cookies

Just like the family in *Six Feet Under*, I grew up right next door to a funeral home, our family business. The caretaker's apartment upstairs was where Sadie and Frank lived. I loved visiting Sadie, and by the age of six, my mom gave me permission to visit by myself.

Even though Sadie's front door was just a minute away, it seemed an epic journey. Out our front door, I would make a sharp left turn and, looking both ways, carefully cross the parking lot to get to the garage where my dad's big green limousines and hearse were stabled. Opening the back door of the mortuary and taking a deep breath, I ran as fast as I could in my white Stride Rite oxfords, past the embalming room, the casket showroom, the chapel with a big stained glass window of the Good Shepherd, "the arrangement room," to finally arrive at the wide carpeted stairs that led to Sadie's apartment. At the top, I would give a light knock on her glass-paneled door. Sadie was always there waiting for me. "There's my little girl." I'd let out my breath and she'd welcome me with a warm hug.

During the hours I was with her, there was an an endless flow of things to talk about: school, plants (she was an early practitioner of rooftop container gardening), my hamster, tap dancing, piano, and accordion lessons. She taught me to knit while I sat in Frank's big, nubby, beige armchair. Sometimes we would go into their neat-as-a-pin bedroom, and while she'd iron, I'd show her my latest tap dance routine and attempted pirouettes.

I learned to bake cookies in her kitchen, with ingredients and amounts that were slightly different each time. We'd set a bowl, wooden spoon, and fork onto the counter, and for measuring, we'd use one of Frank's coffee cups from the cupboard above, and silver teaspoons from the drawer below the counter. Together, we'd cream sugar and butter using the spoon, and a hand-cranked beater until everything was light and fluffy. In a small bowl, we'd fork beat an egg until frothy and add to the creamed sugar. Dry ingredients were next: a coffee cup of flour from a metal tin, a pinch of salt from the round blue box, and baking soda from the little yellow box on the shelf. I'd mix round and round with her big wooden spoon until the dough looked blended and smooth. Sometimes we'd add walnut pieces, and we'd always finish by carefully folding in a cup of Rice Krispies or cornflakes to give our cookies extra crunch.

Dough plops went onto a well-greased baking sheet and into the oven it went. Our noses and eyes told us when the cookies were ready. After they'd cool a bit, I'd have two, washed down with a cup of strong Irish tea laced with plenty of milk and sugar. Then Sadie would cast the yarn on my needles, and I'd happily knit and purl for the rest of the afternoon. When it was time to go, I'd walk down the stairs, not holding my breath this time, and head home to where my mom was just finishing up teaching afternoon piano lessons. Sadie has long since passed away, but whenever I make her cookies, I feel her with me, and I'm still her little girl.

Sadie's Cookies

These cookies are close to the ones I remember making with Sadie. I always think of her when I make them. We baked small batches so I could make more the next time I saw her. It's fine to double the recipe, too.

MAKES 2 DOZEN

INGREDIENTS

½ cup (115 g) butter, softened

⅓ cup (75 g) brown sugar

⅓ cup (66 g) granulated sugar

1 large egg, fork beaten until frothy

½ teaspoon vanilla extract

⅔ cup (96 g) unbleached all-purpose flour

¼ teaspoon salt

½ teaspoon baking soda

1½ to 2 cups (40 to 50 g) cornflakes or Rice Krispies

1 cup (115 g) chopped walnuts (optional)

PROCEDURE

1. Preheat oven to 375°F (190°C).
2. In a medium bowl, cream butter and sugars with a hand mixer until light and fluffy. A stand mixer is fine to use, too.
3. Add egg and vanilla extract, and beat with a mixer until blended. Scrape down the sides of the bowl with a spatula to incorporate all the batter, and mix a bit more.
4. In a small bowl, mix together the flour, salt, and baking soda with a fork or a whisk.
5. Add the dry mixture to the wet mixture, and mix until combined.
6. Add cornflakes or Rice Krispies and optional walnuts, and lightly stir with a spoon to distribute evenly in the batter.
7. Drop from a teaspoon onto parchment-lined or greased cookie sheets.
8. Bake in the preheated oven for about 9 minutes or until they are a nice golden brown. The cookies will flatten out as they bake. Cool for a few minutes before removing from the cookie sheet. Let cool completely before serving.

Childhood Joys

"And how the children love cookies or cakes which have been made especially for them! Not only the eating of these mysterious, delightful creations, but to stand and watch them being made and to wait impatiently what seems ages before these miracles come out of the oven, all brown and fragrant. The memory of these childish joys is never forgotten."

—**Belle DeGraf**
in *Mrs. DeGraf's Cook Book* (1922)

Sadie's Cookies, page 91

Tiny Chocolate Chippers

The smaller these cookies are, the more popular they are—at least in my house. Once, when I placed a mounded-up bowlful of them on the table, directly in front of a friend, she said that they were as addicting as potato chips. You can make their size larger by placing teaspoons of dough onto the cookie sheet, but if you have the time, do try making them the half-teaspoon size.

MAKES ABOUT 11 DOZEN 1¾-INCH (4.5-CM) COOKIES

INGREDIENTS

1 cup (225 g) butter, room temperature

¾ cup (165 g) brown sugar, packed

¾ cup (150 g) granulated sugar

2 large eggs

1 teaspoon vanilla extract

½ teaspoon salt

2¼ cups (328 g) unbleached all-purpose flour

½ teaspoon baking soda

2 cups (350 g) mini-chocolate chips

PROCEDURE

1. Preheat oven to 375°F (190°C).
2. In a large bowl, cream butter and sugars until light and fluffy. A stand mixer is fine to use, too.
3. Add eggs, vanilla, and salt, and mix well. Scrape down the bowl once with a spatula to incorporate all the batter, and mix a bit more.
4. In a medium-small bowl, mix together the flour and baking soda with a fork or a whisk.
5. Add the dry mixture to the wet mixture, and mix until combined.
6. Stir in the mini-chocolate chips until they are evenly distributed.
7. Fill a ½ teaspoon measuring spoon with dough, and push it off with your finger or a spoon onto greased or parchment-lined cookie sheets. For larger cookies, use a teaspoon of dough. Leave about 1½ inches (3 to 4 cm) between the cookies.
8. Bake in the preheated oven for about 9 minutes. They are done when they are golden brown around the edges.
9. Remove from oven. Let cool for a minute. With a spatula, remove the cookies from the pan and place on a cooling rack. If you are using parchment paper, you can carefully slide the entire sheet of parchment paper with cookies on top to a cooling rack.

Fudgy Brownies

Fudgy or cakey. Everyone seems to have an opinion on what the perfect brownie is. My dad liked his slightly fudgy, so that's how we made them. Brownies are always good topped with a scoop of vanilla ice cream, but my chocolate-loving dad was known to eat them with a scoop of rocky road ice cream.

MAKES 24 2-INCH (ABOUT 5-CM) SQUARE BROWNIES

INGREDIENTS

4 large eggs

1 cup (92 g) Dutch Process cocoa powder

½ teaspoon espresso powder (optional)

½ teaspoon salt

2 teaspoons vanilla extract

1 cup (225 g) butter

2 cups (400 g) granulated sugar

1 cup (146 g) unbleached all-purpose flour

½ teaspoon aluminum-free baking powder

1 cup (115 g) roughly chopped walnuts (optional)

PROCEDURE

1. Preheat oven to 350°F (180°C). Butter a 9-by-13-inch (23-by-33-cm) ovenproof baking dish.
2. In a large bowl, crack the eggs. Add the cocoa powder, espresso powder (if using), salt, and vanilla, and mix with a beater until smooth. A stand mixer is fine to use but all the other additions will be with a spoon.
3. Put the butter and sugar into a medium-small saucepan. Turn the heat to low and stir until the butter is melted and the sugar is combined. Remove from heat and let cool for a minute or two.
4. Add the slightly cooled butter and sugar mixture to the egg-and-cocoa mixture. With a spoon, stir until smooth.
5. In a small bowl, mix the flour and baking powder together with a fork or a whisk. Add the dry ingredients into the wet mixture, and stir gently with a spoon until smooth.
6. Stir in the optional walnuts.
7. With a rubber or silicone spatula, spread the batter on the greased 9-by-13-inch (23-by-33-cm) baking dish.
8. Bake in the preheated oven for 25 to 30 minutes until a toothpick comes out clean or with just a few moist crumbs. Don't overcook.
9. Remove from the oven. Cool in the pan on a rack.

Mystery Squash Cookies

Those who have eaten these cookies have been at a loss to figure out what their main ingredient is. They are totally surprised to learn that it is baked squash that gives them their creamy texture. Some have even mistaken them for sweet truffles. Those who are both gluten- and dairy-free can enjoy this sweet little treat, too.

MAKES ABOUT 2 DOZEN COOKIES

INGREDIENTS
½ cup baked winter squash, yam, sweet potato, or pumpkin

1 large egg yolk, beaten

1½ cups (168 g) almond meal

¾ cup (150 g) granulated sugar

1 teaspoon vanilla extract

Zest of one lemon

COATING
Unsweetened chocolate powder

Finely ground coffee, topped with a chocolate-covered coffee bean

Ground cloves mixed with some granulated sugar

Pine nuts

Unsweetened shredded coconut

PROCEDURE
1. Put all the ingredients in a bowl and mix together with a fork until smooth.
2. Cover and refrigerate for about 30 minutes.
3. With clean hands, take teaspoon-size plops of the mixture, and lightly form into walnut-size spheres.
4. Roll the balls in one or more of the coating options.
5. When ready to bake, preheat oven to 350°F (180°C). Place them on a parchment-covered baking sheet or greased cookie tin, and bake for 15 to 20 minutes. Let cool completely.

What Is Enough?

It seems we have lost sight of what is enough. Plates, appetites, and waistlines have increased with supersize portions. In a recent conversation with a cookbook editor, I learned that pie recipes are being updated in new editions of some classic twentieth-century cookbooks because recipes from the 1950s, 60s, and beyond do not fill the larger-sized pie pans of the twenty-first century. Just because it's on the plate does not mean that we have to clean the plate. We can use a smaller plate, one that in my mom's and grandmother's time would have been called a luncheon plate, and arrange a reasonable amount of food on it.

Food can be a means of solace—a way to feed the soul and the emptiness we may feel during times of emotional challenge. Of course, comfort food can fit that bill, but after we have finished a heaping bowl of mashed potatoes or ice cream, the hole is still there, and we look to the next thing to mask it. I love to cook and bake, and have found by making and giving extra to others, a part of that emptiness and wanting is satisfied. When I think of others first, many times I am able to distance myself from an occasional pity party. Knocking on the door of neighbors, especially those who may be homebound or lonely, with a smile and plate of cookies, may be the highlight of their day, and the best part of mine, too.

Pear Berry Pie

I like to pick late summer blackberries and mix them with the first fragrant pears of the fall. When the season for fresh berries has passed, I use frozen berries so I can make this pie in the wintertime when my favorite Comice pears show up at the market. Thawed berries make a filling that is too juicy, so be sure to use them frozen. Pears ripen from the inside out. There should be a slight give at the top near the stem to let you know that it is just about ready to eat. If the pear is completely soft, you may find yourself cutting into fruit that is well past its prime.

MAKES ONE 9-INCH DEEP-DISH PIE

INGREDIENTS

5 large (about 5 cups) ripe pears (skin on), quartered and cored

1 cup (about 144 g) blackberries, fresh or unthawed frozen

½ cup (100 g) granulated sugar

¼ cup (56 g) packed brown sugar

¼ teaspoon salt

¾ teaspoon cinnamon

2 gratings nutmeg

Small squeeze of ½ a lemon

1 to 2 tablespoons (15 to 30 ml) pear brandy (optional)

½ cup (73 g) unbleached all-purpose flour

1 recipe double-crust pie dough (recipe follows)

2 teaspoons butter, chopped into little pieces

1 to 2 teaspoons granulated sugar, for sprinkling on top of the pie

EGG WASH

1 egg white plus 2 tablespoons (30 ml) water, fork beaten

CONTINUED

1. Slice pears into ½-inch (1-cm) slices or chunk them up into pieces you can comfortably get into your mouth.

2. In a large mixing bowl, place all the ingredients, except for the butter and sugar topping, and mix lightly until most of the surfaces are covered.

3. Pour the mixture into an unbaked pie crust, and dot with butter.

4. Roll out the remaining dough, lay it over the fruit, and cut 5 to 6 vents on top, or make a lattice top. Trim the excess dough from the edges and crimp.

5. Cover the pie and chill in the refrigerator while you preheat the oven to 425°F (220°C).

6. Lightly brush some of the egg white wash over the entire pie, including the edges. Sprinkle on the sugar evenly and bake on middle rack of preheated oven for 20 minutes.

7. Reduce the heat to 375°F (190°C) and bake for 35 to 40 minutes longer, until you see some bubbling coming through the vents. If the top of the pie looks like it is browning too quickly, cover with a piece of foil, turned shiny side down, with a vent torn in the middle and continue baking.

8. Cool the pie for at least an hour so it can set up before eating.

Art of the Pie Dough

Use this dough for sweet or savory pies.

INGREDIENTS

2½ cups (363 g) unbleached all-purpose flour, use dip and sweep method

½ teaspoon salt

8 tablespoons (112 g) salted or unsalted butter, cut into tablespoon-size pieces

8 tablespoons (112 g) rendered leaf lard, cut into tablespoon-size pieces

½ cup ice water (118 ml) plus 1 to 2 tablespoons (15 to 30 ml) more as needed

Additional flour for rolling out dough

PROCEDURE

1. Put all ingredients but the ice water in a large bowl.
2. With clean hands, quickly smoosh the mixture together, or use a pastry blender with an up and down motion, until the ingredients look like cracker crumbs with lumps the size of peas and almonds. The lumps make flakey pies.
3. Sprinkle ice water over the mixture and stir lightly with a fork.
4. Squeeze a handful of dough to see if it holds together. Mix in more water as needed.
5. Divide dough in half and make two chubby discs about 5 inches (12 cm) across.
6. Wrap discs separately in plastic wrap, and chill for 20 minutes to an hour. Dough may be pre-made and frozen, and defrosted before use.

Note If you prefer to make an all-butter crust, omit the leaf lard and use 14 tablespoons (196 g) butter.

Art of the Pie Dough, page 103

Our Favorite Biscotti, page 106

Our Favorite Biscotti

When I was growing up in Santa Barbara, I often heard my mom and grandmother say that the way to a man's heart was through his stomach. A batch of this biscotti was put to that test when I shipped a shoebox full to wuzband #3 during our courting days. Soon after they arrived, I got an email reply saying, "You *do* make good biscotti." I had told him that I did, and his words warmed my heart and brought a smile to my face. A few a few months later he proposed to me and I continued to make them for us to enjoy together. Courting or not, biscotti are a perfect little treat any time of the day. I like to dunk mine in a mug of coffee, and they are a very easy snack to take on the road for a quick nibble, too. I've been making this recipe for over thirty years and it always gets compliments from family and friends.

MAKES ABOUT 2 DOZEN

INGREDIENTS

1⅓ cups (140 g) almonds

2 ¾ cups (400 g) unbleached all-purpose flour

1⅔ cups (266 g) granulated sugar

½ teaspoon salt

1 teaspoon aluminum-free baking powder

1 teaspoon anise seed (optional)

Zest of one lemon, orange, and lime (If you don't have all three, don't worry, but do try to use at least one)

3 large eggs plus 3 yolks

1 teaspoon vanilla extract

1. Preheat the oven to 350°F (180°C). Place the almonds on a baking sheet and toast for 10 to 15 minutes. Let them cool.
2. In a large bowl or bowl of a stand mixer, mix the flour, sugar, salt, baking powder, optional anise, and zest.
3. In a medium bowl, whisk the eggs, yolks, and vanilla together until mixed.
4. Pour the egg mixture into the dry mixture and beat on medium with an electric beater or stand mixer until nearly mixed.
5. Add the almonds and mix again until everything just comes together. Don't be tempted to overmix.
6. Turn the dough onto a lightly floured board and knead in everything that was left in the bowl.
7. Divide the dough into three pieces and shape each into cylinders about 10-by-2 inches (25-by-5 cm).
8. Put the cylinders on a greased or parchment-covered cookie sheet with about 4 inches (10 cm) between each.
9. Bake in preheated oven for 45 minutes.
10. Remove from oven and let cool for 10 to 15 minutes.
11. Lower the oven temperature to 300°F (150°C).
12. Set a cylinder on a cutting board and, with a sharp knife, cut a 1-inch-wide (2.5 cm) piece on the diagonal. Repeat with the other two cylinders.
13. Place the slices on the cookie sheet and bake at 300°F (150°C) for another 10 to 15 minutes, depending on how firm you like your biscotti.
14. Remove from oven. Let cool. Store in an airtight container.

Butter Wrappers My mom and grandmother taught me to save the paper that butter is wrapped in, store it in the fridge, and use it to grease baking dishes. I've also been known to use my fingers to grease a pan.

My Sweet Sara

Life lessons that define and shape us can also be the ones that shake us to our very core. One day everything seems to be perking along just fine, and then out of the blue we are presented with an unimaginable challenge. With no preparation or warning, it's just not possible to predict how we will react and cope. One of my biggest lessons in life's uncertainties arrived with the birth of my first child, Sara, who was born with severe mental and physical disabilities.

By the time Sara was two, I had lost two pregnancies, Mom had passed away, and my marriage had shattered. I was now the single working mom of a beautiful little girl with extreme challenges. I had no support system to speak of, and was always scrambling to find reliable childcare, so I could work and pay our bills.

Sara couldn't run at the park or play in the waves like I did as a little girl growing up in Santa Barbara but that didn't stop me from helping her to experience as much of the world as she could. Until she weighed fifty pounds, I carried her in a backpack as we did our in-town errands, walked trails, and hiked up small mountains. On warm days, I loaded us into the car for picnics at the beach and lifted her into waves so she could feel their surge. In the garden, I lay her on a quilt right next to me, and talked and sang to her, while I planted and weeded.

A few years later I remarried, and wuzband #2 and I moved to a tiny cabin on the Olympic Peninsula, to build our dream home. It was here that nearly seven years to the day of her birth, Sara's little brother Duncan was born. I was overjoyed when, just a few days after his birth, he could raise his head when placed on his tummy, something that she could still not do at age seven.

As my children grew, I could see that the nearly round-the-clock care Sara required was taking over the wellbeing of our entire family. After many tears and much soul searching, I made the hardest decision of my life—to give my daughter up to foster care. The perfect couple appeared as if they had been waiting for her all along. Sara was welcomed into their home, and their door was always open to me. I am so very grateful for the selfless and devoted care they gave her. In 2016, after a brief and unexpected illness, Sara passed away at the age of thirty-six. I will always cherish the memory of Sara's easy smile, joyful laughter, and the special times we shared together on a blanket, at the beach, in the mountains, and in our backyard.

Sara's Cheesecake

My daughter, Sara, loved this cheesecake, and I made it for her often. Its height is just around 1 inch tall, and perfect to make in my mom's old cake pan, the one with the bottom that drops out. I've never owned a springform pan, but if you have a 9-inch one, that should be about right for this recipe. Before removing the cheesecake from the pan, run a knife around the edge to make sure that the sides don't stick.

SERVES 8

GRAHAM
CRACKER CRUST

1½ cups (10 to 12 crackers) graham cracker crumbs

⅓ cup (67 g) granulated sugar

⅓ cup (75 g) melted butter

CHEESECAKE

8 ounces (225 g) cream cheese

A squeeze of ½ lemon, about 1 teaspoon

2 teaspoons vanilla extract

2 large eggs, fork beaten

¾ cup (150 g) granulated sugar

TOPPING

1 cup (245 g) sour cream

1 heaping tablespoon granulated sugar

1 teaspoon vanilla extract

PROCEDURE

1. Preheat oven to 350°F (180°C)
2. Buzz up the graham crackers in a food processor, or smash with the back of a spoon until they are the size of coarse salt. Mix with sugar and melted butter. Spread the crumb-butter mixture evenly over the bottom of the cake pan, and press down lightly.
3. Bake for 8 to 10 minutes. Remove from oven and set aside.
4. Put the cream cheese, lemon juice, vanilla, eggs, and sugar in a medium-size bowl, and beat on high with a hand mixer, or in a stand mixer on medium high, until light and fluffy.
5. Pour into the graham cracker crust and bake for 20 minutes. Remove from oven and cool for 5 minutes.
6. Place the sour cream, sugar, and vanilla in a medium-size bowl, and mix with a hand or stand mixer, on medium until smooth. Pour topping over cheesecake and bake for 10 minutes longer.
7. Remove from oven and let cool for an hour. Then place in refrigerator to set for at least 5 hours, or overnight.

From the Land

My Garden

I literally have put down roots on every piece of land where I have lived. Trees, roses, shrubs, herbs, vegetables; I have a very primal need to have my hands in the soil, plant seeds, and watch them sprout and grow. In the spring, I pat soil over seeds and say the words "grow and prosper." Planting and caring for a vegetable garden is a practice of trust, hope, patience, plus a big dose of magic. It feeds my soul in many ways.

In times of happiness, as well as great sorrow, my garden is where I have turned to mark personal passages. It is where I planted a rose to celebrate a marriage, and trees to mark my children's births. It is where I found solace when my mom passed away, I lost two pregnancies, and weathered the breakup of my first marriage, all within one year. I have no idea if it was my tears or the weather, but the harvest during that year of great loss included dinner-plate-size broccoli heads; enough peas, beans, and greens to share with neighbors; and endless bouquets of sweet peas, a flower both Mom and I loved.

When I moved to a tiny 325-square-foot cabin, my garden gave me a much-needed sense of space to balance out the tight quarters I shared with my second wuzband, and two small children. After building a post-and-beam house with our own hands, the cabin became the guesthouse when family and friends visited us. I enjoyed inviting them to the garden to help pick fresh lettuce, beans, and tomatoes for our salads.

During the years I spent living in a treehouse perched on a mountainside, I settled for container gardening. The steep terrain of my 10 acres was populated by rocky soil and tall cedar trees, making it virtually impossible to scratch out any sunny plot for growing. With a deck garden, I could simply walk out my front door and snip off potted herbs and veggies for the kitchen, and flowers for the table.

In my current garden that surrounds Pie Cottage, I have created pocket gardens with herbs and flowers, and a big sunny plot for vegetables. They produce abundantly, and much to the delight of friends and neighbors, there's always extra to share. Good fences and garden harvests make for great neighbors.

Twice-Baked Potatoes with Mushrooms, Broccoli, and Cheese

Baked potato night is a favorite at Pie Cottage. A twice-baked potato takes the simple tuber to new heights. Feel free to adjust the recipe to whatever vegetables you have on hand. Just about anything works when stuffed back into the potato jackets. Add a salad to this simple meal and you're good to go. Choose potatoes that are similar in size so that the baking time will be the same for each of them.

SERVES 4

INGREDIENTS

4 medium to large baking potatoes such as russets

¼ cup (60 g) butter

1 cup (90 g) small broccoli florets and chopped stems

1 cup (86 g) sliced mushrooms

2 or 3 slices cooked bacon, crumbled (optional)

1 cup (225 g) sour cream or plain yogurt

1½ cups (170 g) grated sharp cheddar cheese, or a mixture of cheddar and Parmigiano-Reggiano cheese

1 teaspoon salt

⅛ teaspoon freshly ground black pepper

Dash of paprika

Note One potato, two potato, three potato more . . . you can easily adjust your fillings to fit the number of potatoes you want to stuff.

---

1. Preheat oven to 425°F (220°C). Pierce each potato in several places with a fork, and place potatoes on baking sheet. Bake in preheated oven for about an hour or until you can easily pierce the flesh with a fork. Take the potatoes out of the oven and turn down the oven to 400°F (205°C).

2. Melt half the butter in a sauté pan over medium heat, and cook broccoli for about 5 minutes or until almost tender. Add mushrooms and cook until they begin to soften.

3. Slice off the top of each potato, scoop out the insides with a spoon, and place in a medium-size bowl. You may want to wrap the potato in a towel if it is really hot so as not to burn your hand. Save the potato shells and tops.

4. Add the remaining butter, and mash with a fork or a potato masher.

5. To the mashed potatoes, add the sautéed vegetables, bacon (if using), sour cream or yogurt, cheese, salt, and pepper, and mix until everything is well distributed.

6. Refill the potato shells with the mixture. They will be overflowing! If there is extra, pile it carefully on the potato tops.

7. Sprinkle with a little paprika and bake in the oven for 15 minutes more.

Solitary Eaters

By the time lunch rolls around on days that I have missed breakfast, I sometimes have to restrain myself from standing in front of the refrigerator as I mindlessly graze directly from the shelves. You never do that, right? With family grown and out of the house, sometimes I need to give myself a "pep talk for solitary eaters," as Mollie Katzen aptly calls it in her book, *The Enchanted Broccoli Forest*. So here's my pep talk. It takes less than thirty seconds to place a meal, even if it is leftovers from last night's supper, on a pretty plate, get out a proper cloth napkin from the drawer, and sit at the table, untethered from computer and phone, to eat. I can guarantee that everything will still be waiting for us when we've finished.

Twice-Baked Potatoes with Mushrooms, Broccoli, and Cheese, page 114

Good and Garlicky Potato Salad, page 118

Good and Garlicky Potato Salad

Potatoes. I grow them. I eat them. I love them. It must be some throwback to my Celtic roots. This salad is one delicious way to enjoy them. If you don't have Yellow Finns, new red potatoes will do nicely. I don't peel my potatoes, but you certainly can if that's how you like them best.

SERVES 6 TO 8

SALAD

8 medium Yellow Finn or red potatoes

3 large hard-boiled eggs, coarsely chopped

1 stalk celery, finely chopped

DRESSING

1 large clove garlic (feel free to use more if you are a garlic lover)

¼ cup (60 ml) artisan apple cider vinegar, such as Bragg's

¼ teaspoon salt

¼ cup (60 ml) olive oil

2 tablespoons (30 ml) mayonnaise

½ teaspoon dried oregano

¼ teaspoon dried thyme

⅛ teaspoon freshly ground black pepper

¾ teaspoon Dijon mustard

PROCEDURE

1. Place potatoes in a lidded saucepan and cover with about 2 inches (5 cm) of water. Bring to a boil. Cover and lower the heat. Simmer for 15 minutes until the potatoes can be pierced easily with a fork but still hold their shape. Drain off the water.

2. While the potatoes cook, make the dressing. Place the garlic, vinegar, salt, olive oil, mayonnaise, oregano, thyme, pepper, and mustard in a lidded jar and shake well.

3. Drain the potatoes, and chop, slice, and dice them into a variety of shapes and sizes.

4. Add eggs and celery, and gently toss.

5. Pour the dressing over, and toss again. Serve warm.

Potato Curry with Spinach and Mushrooms

I like the way this recipe combines potatoes, harvested from under the soil, with leafy green spinach or chard, harvested from above. If your spice rack is missing mustard and cumin seeds, turmeric and coriander, add two tablespoons of curry powder in their place, and continue on.

SERVES 4 TO 6

INGREDIENTS

3 tablespoons (45 ml) safflower oil

1 tablespoon whole mustard seeds

1 tablespoon whole cumin seeds

2 teaspoons turmeric

½ teaspoon ground coriander

⅛ teaspoon cayenne, or more if you like it really spicy

1 teaspoon salt

4 medium potatoes, unpeeled and roughly chopped to ½- to 1-inch (1- to 2.5-cm) pieces

1 medium onion, chopped

1 cup (250 ml) water

1 bunch fresh spinach or chard, washed and coarsely chopped

¾ pound (350 g) sliced mushrooms

1 cup (225 g) plain yogurt or sour cream, plus more for serving

PROCEDURE

1. Heat oil over medium heat in a Dutch oven or heavy cast-iron skillet with lid.
2. Add the mustard seeds and cumin seeds. The seeds will pop a bit. Add the turmeric, coriander, cayenne, and salt. Stir around quickly until blended.
3. Add potatoes and onions, and stir until well coated.
4. Add the water, cover, and let cook for about 20 minutes until potatoes are tender. Add more water if needed.
5. Stir in the spinach or chard and cook a few minutes more until wilted.
6. Stir in mushrooms and cook a few minutes more.
7. Add yogurt or sour cream, and cook, stirring occasionally.
8. Serve with an extra dollop of yogurt or sour cream on top.

Roasted Root Vegetables

Roasting vegetables is an easy way to use up all the odds and ends in our vegetable drawers and the long roast brings out the flavors hiding inside. Serve them drizzled with balsamic vinegar, or sprinkled with a bit of grated Parmigiano-Reggiano cheese. It's very nice to have roasted veggies on hand in the fridge to add to a soup or stew, so you may want to double the recipe. They'll be good for at least three days.

SERVES 4 TO 6

INGREDIENTS

4 to 6 cups (1 to 2 lbs or 450 to 900 g) combination potatoes, onions, carrots, parsnips, and leeks

1 whole head garlic, broken up into cloves

2 tablespoons (30 ml) olive oil

1 teaspoon salt, plus more to taste

Freshly ground black pepper, to taste

Several sprigs of fresh rosemary, thyme, or other herbs of choice

Balsamic vinegar (optional)

Parmigiano-Reggiano cheese, grated (optional)

PROCEDURE

1. Preheat oven to 350°F (180°C).
2. Chop and cut the potatoes, onions, carrots, parsnips, and leeks into uniform-size pieces that are not too large and not too small. Place in a large bowl. Add the garlic cloves.
3. Add the olive oil, and salt and pepper to taste, and toss until everything is well coated.
4. Turn into a baking dish and tuck in herb sprigs here and there.
5. Roast for 90 minutes, stirring and turning the vegetables occasionally.
6. Continue roasting until you can easily pierce the flesh of the potatoes with a fork.
7. Add more salt and pepper to taste. Sprinkle on some optional balsamic vinegar or Parmigiano-Reggiano and serve.

Corn, Pepper, Tomato, and Sausage Pie

During my early years as a California transplant to the Pacific Northwest, I had no idea what would grow in my first vegetable gardens. I planted broccoli and cabbage, crops that thrive in cooler weather, and corn, peppers, and tomatoes that do well in hot weather. I learned that the success of a harvest is different from year to year. One summer my harvest looked like the centerfold of a garden magazine, and I had plenty of tomatoes, corn, and peppers to share. When possible, use fresh vegetables in this filling, but canned corn and tomatoes will work nicely, too. Top with home-made dough, or use store-bought dough if that is easiest for you.

SERVES 6 TO 8

INGREDIENTS

1½ tablespoons (22 ml) olive oil

3 cloves garlic, minced

½ large red pepper, chopped

½ large green pepper, chopped

3 large ears of sweet corn, husked and sliced off the cob to total about 2 cups kernels, or one 15-ounce can (425 grams total)

⅓ cup roasted tomatoes (see sidebar on how to roast tomatoes on page 150), or ¾ cup canned plum tomatoes, chopped

1 teaspoon fresh or dried herbs of your choice, such as oregano, thyme, basil, or rosemary

1 heaping tablespoon marinated red peppers, roughly chopped, plus a little of the oil

3 tablespoons (36 g) grated Parmigiano-Reggiano cheese

1 pound (450 g) Italian mild or hot sausage meat (remove casings if using links)

Salt and freshly ground black pepper to taste

1 recipe Art of the Pie Dough (see page 103) or store-bought dough

EGG WASH

1 large egg with 2 teaspoons water, fork beaten

1. Heat olive oil over medium heat in a heavy cast-iron skillet or Dutch oven.
2. Add garlic and sauté for 20 to 30 seconds while stirring. Add the red and green peppers, and sauté for about 5 minutes, stirring occasionally. Add the corn, tomatoes, and herbs, and sauté for another 5 minutes, stirring occasionally.
3. Stir in the marinated peppers and their oil. Remove from heat and turn into a medium bowl. Add the grated cheese and set aside.
4. Replace the skillet on the stove over medium heat, and place the sausage meat in the pan. If using link sausage, remove the casings. Break the sausage up into bite-size pieces with a knife or clean fingers. Cook over medium heat until the pink has faded and the sausages are slightly golden brown. Stir occasionally to make sure that all sides have cooked. Remove from the heat.
5. Turn the cooked sausages into the vegetable mixture, and set the entire mixture aside to cool, while you make the dough. If making at home, follow the recipe for Art of the Pie Dough on page 103.
6. Roll out the bottom crust and place in a 9-inch (23-cm) deep-dish pie pan. Spoon or pour the cooled vegetable and sausage mixture evenly into the bottom crust.
7. Roll out the top crust and place on top of filling. Trim the edge of top and bottom doughs to about ½ inch (1 cm) over the edge of the pie pan. Roll the edges up around the pie. Finish edge with crimp or flute. Cut a few vents through the top dough.
8. Place the pie in the refrigerator to chill for at least 20 minutes or 5 minutes in the freezer.
9. When ready to bake, preheat the oven to 440°F (225°C). Just before baking, paint the egg wash on top of the pie all over, including the edges. Bake in preheated oven for 20 minutes.
10. Turn the heat down to 375°F (190°C) and continue to bake for 40 minutes more.

Corn, Pepper, Tomato, and Sausage Pie, page 122

Baked Winter Squash

I like seeing the many colors, shapes, and varieties of winter squash offered at farmers' markets and in produce sections at the grocery store. They store easily, are not fussy to bake, and are lovely filled with stuffing for a simple supper.

SERVES 4 TO 6

INGREDIENTS

1 medium (about 2½ lbs or 1 kg) acorn or butternut squash

1 stuffing recipe of choice (recipes on pages 127–131)

PROCEDURE

1. Preheat oven to 400°F (200°C).
2. Cut squash in half. Scoop out the pulp and seeds with a spoon.
3. Put about ¼ inch (5 mm) of water in an ovenproof casserole. Set the squash in the casserole with the cut side down.
4. Bake for 20 minutes. While baking, prepare the stuffing of your choice.
5. Remove from oven, turn the partially baked squash halves over, and stuff. Return to oven and bake filled cut side up about 20 to 30 minutes more.

Note Add more baking time for larger squashes.

Stuffed Peppers

Peppers are easy to make and can adapt to whatever filling you would like to stuff in them. Try a different stuffing each time you make them until you settle on one you like best.

MAKES 6

INGREDIENTS

1 stuffing recipe of your choice (recipes follow)

6 large green, yellow, orange, or red peppers

Grated cheese of choice, optional

PROCEDURE

1. Make the stuffing recipe and set aside.
2. Preheat oven to 350°F (180°C).
3. Remove the pepper tops and seeds.
4. Fill the pepper with the stuffing of choice.
5. Put ½ inch (1 cm) of water in an ovenproof casserole. Set the peppers in and bake in preheated oven for 20 minutes.
6. Remove from the oven and sprinkle on some optional grated cheese. Return to oven and continue to bake until the cheese melts.

Apple Nut Stuffing

MAKES ABOUT 3½ CUPS

INGREDIENTS

2 to 3 apples, sliced or chopped to total about 2 cups

¾ cup (110 g) raisins

1 cup (115 g) walnuts, chopped

½ cup (120 ml) grade A or B maple syrup

1 teaspoon cinnamon

¼ teaspoon allspice

Fresh nutmeg, a grating or two

¼ teaspoon salt

PROCEDURE

1. Place apples and raisins in a saucepan with a little water so they won't stick. Cook over medium heat for about 10 minutes until the apples soften. Remove from heat.
2. Add walnuts, maple syrup, cinnamon, allspice, nutmeg, and salt. Taste and add more maple syrup or salt to your taste.

CONTINUED

Rice Stuffing

MAKES ABOUT 3 CUPS

INGREDIENTS

1½ tablespoons (21 ml) olive oil

½ pound (225 g) pork sausage meat

3 cloves garlic, minced

1 medium onion, chopped small

½ medium red pepper, chopped

½ teaspoon oregano

½ teaspoon thyme

1 teaspoon salt

1½ cups (375 g) cooked rice

PROCEDURE

1. In a cast-iron skillet or sauté pan, heat ½ tablespoon (7 ml) olive oil over medium heat. Add sausage and break up with a spoon while it browns. Drain on a plate lined with a paper towel and set aside.
2. In a cast-iron skillet or sauté pan, heat the remaining 1 tablespoon (14 ml) olive oil over medium-low heat. Add garlic, onions, red pepper, oregano, thyme, and salt, and cook until the onion is soft.
3. Add the cooked rice and sausage, and stir to mix. Remove from heat.

Bread Stuffing

MAKES ABOUT 5 CUPS

INGREDIENTS

2 tablespoons (30 g) butter

3 cloves garlic, minced

1 medium onion, chopped small

2 celery stalks, sliced in ¼-inch (5-mm) half-moons

1 cup (70 g) sliced mushrooms

1 teaspoon salt

1 teaspoon parsley

¼ teaspoon sage

¼ teaspoon rosemary

1 teaspoon thyme

6 slices bread, toasted and cut into 1-inch (2.5-cm) squares, or about 4 cups of leftover corn bread

½ cup (120 ml) chicken stock

½ cup (65 g) roughly chopped dried cherries or cranberries

PROCEDURE

1. In a cast-iron skillet or sauté pan, heat the butter over medium-low heat.
2. Add the garlic, onion, and celery, and cook until the onion is soft and transparent.
3. Add the mushrooms, salt, parsley, sage, rosemary, and thyme and cook for a few minutes more.
4. Add the bread, chicken stock, and dried cherries, and cook on stovetop for another few minutes. Remove from heat.

Note Feel free to add a cup or so of cooked pork sausage.

CONTINUED

Sour Cream Rice Stuffing

MAKES ABOUT 4 CUPS

INGREDIENTS

½ cup (115 ml) sour cream or plain yogurt

1 cup (100 g) grated Parmigiano-Reggiano cheese

¾ teaspoon salt

1 teaspoon thyme

1 teaspoon parsley

2 tablespoons (30 ml) butter or olive oil

3 cloves garlic, minced

½ medium onion, chopped small

1 large stalk celery, sliced in ¼-inch (5-mm) half-moons

¾ cup (55 g) roughly chopped mushrooms

¼ cup (40 g) sliced almonds (optional)

1½ cups (about 375 g) cooked rice

PROCEDURE

1. Mix together the sour cream or yogurt, Parmigiano-Reggiano, salt, thyme and parsley, and set aside.
2. In a cast-iron skillet or sauté pan, heat the butter or oil over medium-low heat.
3. Add garlic, onion, and celery and sauté until the onion is soft and transparent.
4. When nearly done, add the mushrooms and optional almonds, and cook another minute.
5. Remove from the heat and stir in the cooked rice and the sour cream sauce.

Potato Cheese Stuffing

MAKES ABOUT 4 CUPS

INGREDIENTS

2 cups (310 g) cooked potatoes

1 cup (225 ml) sour cream or plain yogurt

1 cup (150 g) crumbled goat cheese

½ cup (70 g) crumbled Stilton or other blue cheese

3 scallions, whites and greens, thinly sliced

2 tablespoons chopped fresh parsley

½ teaspoon salt

½ teaspoon freshly ground black pepper

1 teaspoon garlic powder

4 slices cooked bacon, chopped small (optional)

PROCEDURE

1. In a medium bowl, mash the potatoes.
2. Mix in the sour cream or yogurt, goat cheese, and Stilton cheese.
3. Add the scallion, parsley, salt, pepper, garlic powder, and optional bacon. Mix to combine.

How to Roast Garlic

It takes just one clove of garlic to grow an entire head. That little pointed clove, tucked down into the earth in the fall, emerges nine months later as a full head. I plant at least one hundred individual cloves in hopes of harvesting one hundred heads of "the stinking rose" at summer's end. This many may seem like a lot to you, but in my house, that entire harvest will be eaten before the year's end. An entire head might go into Duncan's Breakfast Hash (see page 18) and, if making marinara sauce from a wheelbarrow full of homegrown tomatoes, thirty heads are just about right. I like to roast garlic and spread it on toast like butter. It's delicious. The roasted heads will last in the refrigerator for about two weeks, and can be frozen, and added to soups, stews, stuffings, eggs, or Almost Hummus (see page 60).

INGREDIENTS   Garlic heads
                   Olive oil

PROCEDURE
1. Preheat oven to 375°F (190°C).
2. Peel off any loose papery skin on large heads of garlic, but if you forget this step it will be okay, too. Cut off about ¼ to ½ inch (5 to 10 mm) from the top of the entire head so you can see all the little cloves inside. Repeat with each head you will be baking. Don't be skimpy—in fact, you might want to double the amount you had planned on baking because once you taste roast garlic, you will wish you had baked more.
3. Place the garlic heads in a bowl. Drizzle some olive oil over, and stir or massage to make sure the oil covers the outside.
4. Place the oiled heads cut side up in a baking dish or a pie pan. Drizzle a little more oil over the top so that it soaks down into the cloves.
5. Cover tightly with a sheet of aluminum foil.
6. Bake for 90 minutes or longer until the cloves are tender. The longer you bake it, the darker the cloves will get, and the deeper and richer the flavor will be. The kitchen will smell delicious, too.
7. Cool and serve. Squeeze out individual cloves onto bread and spread like butter.

Zucchini Frittata Casserole

In the fall of my junior year of high school, my dad suddenly passed away. He was 54. Our lives were very lonely without him, so with Thanksgiving coming up, Mom accepted an invitation for us to spend it in San Francisco at the home of some of their oldest and dearest friends, to help ease our sadness and loss. This frittata casserole served that day was like nothing I had tasted before. It was so good, I asked if I might have the recipe to take home. Months later when I made it for a gathering honoring my dad, my Italian godfather said, "That's just how my mama used to make it." For this recipe, use store-bought Italian-style breadcrumbs.

SERVES 8-10

INGREDIENTS

2 to 3 medium zucchini, grated

1½ cups (134 g) Italian-style breadcrumbs or gluten-free Italian-seasoned breadcrumbs

1½ cups (150 g) grated Parmigiano-Reggiano cheese

2 medium onions, chopped

3 cloves garlic, minced

1½ tablespoons Italian seasoning

1 teaspoon salt

1 teaspoon freshly ground black pepper

7 large eggs, lightly beaten with a whisk

1 cup (240 ml) olive oil

PROCEDURE

1. Preheat oven to 325°F (160°C).
2. In a large bowl, mix together the zucchini, breadcrumbs, cheese, onions, garlic, Italian seasoning, salt, and pepper with a spoon.
3. In a medium-size bowl, whisk or fork beat the eggs, add the olive oil, and whisk again. Add to zucchini mixture, and mix to combine.
4. Turn into a 12-by-15-inch (31-by-38-cm) baking dish and bake for 50 to 60 minutes until it is a nice golden brown on top. Let sit for about 10 minutes to let the bubbling olive oil settle back into the casserole.

Note Several bunches of fresh spinach (or a package of frozen) that have been cooked, drained, squeezed, and chopped can be substituted for the zucchini.

Spinach, Onion, and Cheese Tart

By the strictest definition, a pie with only a bottom crust is a tart. Janet Clarkson writes in her book, *Pie: A Global History*, of the lively debate in the 1920s in which "the *Oxford English Dictionary*, the erudite nineteenth century readers of *The Times*, and the Supreme Court of the United States fail(ed) to reach consensus on the question, 'What, exactly, is a pie?'" Since they couldn't decide, go ahead and call this simple dish by whichever name you prefer.

INGREDIENTS

½ recipe Art of the Pie Dough (see page 103) or store-bought dough

2 tablespoons (30 g) butter

1 large onion, thinly sliced

½ teaspoon salt

1 bunch spinach, trimmed of stems, washed and patted dry

2 large eggs

1½ cups (350 ml) half and half, or a combination of half milk and half heavy cream

2 tablespoons Dijon mustard

½ cup (60 g) crumbled goat cheese, or grated Swiss cheese

1 tablespoon chopped pickled red peppers in oil

PROCEDURE

1. Pre-bake a crust in a tart pan and set aside. See directions on how to proceed on page 103.
2. Preheat the oven to 375°F (190°C).
3. In a medium-size skillet, melt the butter over medium-low heat. Add the onions and salt, and cook for about 5 minutes. Add the spinach a handful at a time. Stir it around in the pan until it is wilted and soft. Set aside.
4. Break the eggs into a medium-size bowl, and fork beat or whisk. Add half and half mixture, and mustard, and whisk again.
5. Lay the spinach and onion evenly on the bottom of the partially baked tart shell, sprinkle the cheese on top, and pour the egg mixture over.
6. Bake in the preheated oven for 35 to 40 minutes. Let cool for 5 minutes and then serve.

CONTINUED

To Make a Partially Baked Pastry Shell

1. Roll out pie dough, gently place in a chilled pie pan, and flute or crimp the edges.
2. With a fork, evenly prick the bottom and sides of the dough.
3. Cover with plastic and place in freezer until very well-chilled. This will help with the inevitable shrinkage of the crust during the bake.
4. Remove plastic wrap and cover dough with a sheet of parchment paper that is cut about 2 inches (5 cm) larger than your pie pan. Cut the paper large as you will be lifting out hot pie weights and you don't want them to spill into the crust or onto the floor.
5. Place 1 to 1½ cups of dry beans or rice on top of the parchment.
6. In an oven preheated to 375°F (190°C), bake the pie shell for 20 to 25 minutes.
7. Remove from oven and carefully take out the parchment paper and pie weights. If a bit of the dough has stuck onto the backside of the parchment, now is the time you can carefully scrape it off and gently pat it back onto the spot in the crust where it came from. Let cool.

Brussels, Bacon, and Blue

The three B's in music are Bach, Beethoven, and Brahms. On my Thanksgiving table, they are Brussels sprouts, bacon, and blue cheese. I could eat this entire recipe by myself without feeling the tiniest pang of guilt.

SERVES 6 TO 8

INGREDIENTS

2 pounds (900 g) Brussels sprouts (about 6 to 7 cups)

¼ teaspoon smoked paprika

¼ teaspoon salt

¼ teaspoon freshly ground black pepper

3 to 4 cloves garlic, chopped

¼ teaspoon dried dill (optional)

Sprinkling of cayenne (optional)

¼ cup (40 g) crumbled blue cheese

3 slices bacon, cooked and chopped

2 to 3 tablespoons (30 to 45 g) grated butter or olive oil

PROCEDURE

1. Preheat oven to 375°F (190°C). Grease a large baking dish with butter.
2. Wash the Brussels sprouts and trim off a bit of their ends. Slice the sprouts in half.
3. Lay half of the sliced sprouts in the pan with the cut side up.
4. Mix together the smoked paprika, salt, pepper, garlic, optional dill and cayenne, and sprinkle half of it over the sprouts. Crumble half the blue cheese and half the chopped bacon over the sprouts.
5. Repeat Steps 3 and 4 with the remaining sprouts and toppings.
6. Evenly spread grated butter or olive oil over the top.
7. Bake in preheated oven for 35 to 40 minutes, until the cheese is melted and the sprouts are fork tender.

Spinach Salad with Water Chestnuts and Bacon

This was my mom's favorite salad—I think. But then again, maybe the reason she served it so often was to encourage me to eat my vegetables. The sweet and sour dressing was so good that I was happy to clean my plate and sometimes ask for more. It was on our table at least once a week, and at all of our family gatherings.

SERVES 4 TO 6

INGREDIENTS
2 bunches spinach, trimmed of stems, washed and patted dry

¾ pound (350 g) bean sprouts, rinsed

One 8-ounce (226-g) can sliced water chestnuts, drained

6 to 8 slices bacon, cooked crisp, drained on paper towels, and chopped

DRESSING
1 cup (250 ml) olive oil

½ cup (120 ml) red wine vinegar

⅓ cup (80 g) ketchup (my mom always used Heinz)

⅓ cup (33 g) granulated sugar (optional)

1 medium red onion, grated

Salt and freshly ground black pepper to taste

PROCEDURE
1. Place the spinach into a large mixing bowl.
2. Add the bean sprouts and water chestnuts.
3. Place the olive oil, vinegar, ketchup, optional sugar, grated onion, salt, and pepper in a jar with a lid and shake well.
4. Pour dressing over salad and toss well.
5. Add bacon pieces and toss again lightly. Add salt and pepper to taste.

Spring Pasta with Peas, Mushrooms, and Bacon

Peas love cool weather and are one of the earliest crops to sprout and send up shoots in my garden. After the green vines have flowered and are full of swelling pods, I pick a big bowlful to shell. It does take quite a few shelled pods to yield two cups of peas, but it's an easy chore that young children have fun doing and I find rather meditative. Of course, it's perfectly fine to use frozen peas, too.

SERVES 6

INGREDIENTS

6 pieces bacon, cooked, cooled, and chopped into small pieces (see Baked Up Bacon, page 24)

2 tablespoons (30 g) butter

2 tablespoons (30 g) olive oil

3 cloves garlic, minced

½ pound (225 g) mushrooms, sliced

1 teaspoon salt

½ teaspoon freshly ground black pepper

2 cups (230 g) peas, fresh or frozen

¼ to ½ cup (60 to 120 ml) chicken broth or water

¼ cup (60 ml) half and half or heavy cream

1 pound (450 g) fettuccini pasta

1 cup (100 g) grated Parmigiano-Reggiano cheese

1 handful fresh parsley, chopped

1. Cook the bacon, drain on paper towels, and set aside.
2. Bring a large pot of water to boil.
3. In a wide, heavy skillet, melt the butter and olive oil over medium heat. Add the garlic and let cook for 30 seconds or so, while stirring around with a spoon so it won't burn.
4. Add the mushrooms, salt, and pepper, and sauté for about a minute.
5. Add the peas, and about ¼ cup water or chicken broth. Turn up the heat and cook for 3 to 4 minutes. Add the half and half or cream, and cook for another 2 minutes while stirring. Turn off the heat.
6. Cook the pasta according to the directions on the package, drain, and add to the pan with the vegetables.
7. Sprinkle the cheese and parsley over the top, and toss well with tongs or two forks.
8. Divide evenly on individual plates, and sprinkle each serving with crumbled bacon.
9. Serve with extra Parmigiano-Reggiano, and salt and pepper at the table.

Note In my garden, you'll find one of my favorite peas: the Little Purple Snowpea. The beautiful lavender and purple flowers become tender pods that can be eaten straight off the vine without any cooking. Duncan and his playgroup friends loved to snack on them. I learned from a longtime gardener that "peas like their feet wet and their heads in the sun."

Quick Linguini with Mushroom, Basil, and Garlic

In my home, everyone likes pasta, and I've found it to be a surefire way to get something satisfying on the table without a lot of fussy steps. This simple dish uses an entire head of garlic and is one of the reasons I grow more than one hundred heads each year.

SERVES 4 TO 6

INGREDIENTS

6 tablespoons (90 g) butter

1 head garlic, or at least 10 cloves, minced

1 pound (450 g) mushrooms, sliced

10 to 12 leaves fresh basil, sliced thin, or 1 teaspoon dried

⅓ teaspoon salt

Freshly ground black pepper

2 tablespoons (30 ml) olive oil

½ handful fresh parsley, chopped fine

1 pound (450 g) linguini

Parmigiano-Reggiano cheese, grated

PROCEDURE

1. Fill a large pot ¾ full of water. Add 1½ teaspoons salt, and turn up the heat so that the water will be boiling when it is time to cook the pasta.
2. In a medium saucepan, melt half the butter over medium heat.
3. Add garlic, and cook for a minute while stirring. Don't let it burn.
4. Add mushrooms, basil, and salt, and cook about 5 minutes or until the mushrooms are tender.
5. Add the remaining butter, a few grinds of black pepper, and olive oil. Remove from heat, stir, and set aside.
6. Cook the linguini according to the directions on the package. Drain, rinse briefly in a colander, shake off the excess water, and pour into a serving bowl.
7. Reheat the sauce briefly, pour over the top of the pasta, and toss well.
8. Serve with chopped parsley and grated Parmigiano-Reggiano.

Pasta with Broccoli and Garlic

On Washington's Olympic Peninsula, we have either hot tomato summers or cool broccoli summers. After harvesting the main head of my broccoli plant, it continues to produce smaller side shoots that are just the right size. Add red pepper flakes to this quick dish to make it spicy.

SERVES 6

INGREDIENTS

2 pounds (900 g) broccoli

1 pound (450 g) pasta

¼ cup (60 ml) olive oil

4 to 6 cloves garlic, chopped

Red pepper flakes (optional)

4 anchovy fillets, smooshed with the back of a spoon

Salt and freshly ground black pepper

PROCEDURE

1. Fill a large pot ¾ full of water. Add 1½ teaspoons salt, and turn up the heat so that the water will be boiling when it is time to cook the pasta.
2. Cut off the very bottom stem of the broccoli if it looks dry and tough, and discard. Peel the skin from the stem of the broccoli. Cut the flower head and stem into small pieces.
3. Bring water to a boil in a medium-size pot, add broccoli, cover, and cook for 3 to 5 minutes, until the stem pieces are tender but not mushy. Drain well and set aside.
4. Cook the pasta according to the directions on the package while you go on with the next step.
5. In a wide, heavy skillet, heat the olive oil over medium heat. Add the garlic and the optional red pepper flakes, and let cook for 30 seconds or so, stirring with a spoon.
6. Add the smooshed anchovies to the pan, and stir.
7. Add the cooked broccoli, and cook for 2 minutes while stirring it around so that the pieces get coated with the sauce. Season with salt and pepper.
8. Drain the pasta, add to the pan with the vegetables, toss well with tongs or two forks, and serve.

Quick and Easy Fresh Broccoli Soup

Broccoli has got to be one of the most versatile vegetables ever. It's good raw, sautéed, steamed, and cooks quickly in this simple soup. From start to finish, this fresh soup can be on the table in about 30 minutes. Leftover chicken that has been cut into bite-size pieces is a nice addition to the pot, too.

SERVES 6

INGREDIENTS

1½ pounds (675 g) broccoli

¼ cup (60 ml) olive oil

3 cloves garlic, chopped

¼ cup (50 g) rice

4 cups (1 l) chicken broth

Salt and freshly ground black pepper

½ cup (50 g) grated Parmigiano-Reggiano cheese, for serving

PROCEDURE

1. Cut off the very bottom stems of the broccoli if it looks dry and tough, and discard. Peel the stem of the broccoli. Cut the flower head and stem into smaller pieces.
2. Bring water to a boil in a medium-size pot, add broccoli, cover, and cook for about 3 minutes. Drain and set aside.
3. In a large Dutch oven or 4-quart, lidded pot, heat the olive oil over medium heat, add garlic, and cook for 30 seconds.
4. Add the broccoli and rice and stir for 2 minutes.
5. Add the broth, salt, and pepper, and bring to a boil. Reduce heat, cover, and simmer for about 15 minutes until the broccoli is tender, and the rice is done.
6. Serve as is, or puree in a blender.
7. Serve with grated Parmigiano-Reggiano cheese.

Pesto

The biggest garden I ever tended had twenty large raised beds. Each summer, at least one was packed with lush, leafy green basil plants. Come harvest time, when I pulled up the plants and pinched the leaves off the stems, the tips of my fingers turned nearly black from all the oil they contained. A first of the season pasta with pesto dinner marked the harvest. That dinner is so easy it doesn't really need a recipe. Just cook up your favorite pasta in a big pot, drain, rinse briefly so it won't stick together, place some pasta on each plate, and pass the pesto. Pesto can be used to flavor so many things. A spoonful is an excellent topping for eggs, delicious drizzled on top of ripe tomato slices, and can even be used in place of mayonnaise in sandwiches.

MAKES ABOUT 1 CUP

INGREDIENTS

2 cloves garlic

1 teaspoon salt

3 cups (75 g) packed fresh basil leaves, plucked off stems

2 tablespoons (20 g) pine nuts

½ cup (60 ml) olive oil

½ cup (50 g) grated Parmigiano-Reggiano cheese

1 pound (450 g) pasta

MORTAR METHOD

1. Peel and crush garlic and pound to a paste with the salt. Chop the leaves and add to the mortar along with the pine nuts. Grind and crush until you have a paste. Gradually beat in the oil, beginning with a few drops at a time, to make a thick sauce, and then stir in the cheese.

BLENDER METHOD

1. Put all the ingredients, except cheese, in a blender. Blend, stopping to push down with a rubber spatula until the mixture is thoroughly pureed. Beat in the cheese.

Note Double the recipe and freeze the extra in containers for use all year long. For single servings, freeze in ice cube trays, remove, and store in ziplock bags, or use a 1-cup yogurt container. Be sure to put a date on the bag or the container, too.

How to Roast Tomatoes

During a hot tomato summer with lots of ripe fruit, I roast some so I can enjoy their harvest for a month or two longer. The process takes minimal effort, but gives a big return with intensified tomato flavor. Roasted tomatoes can be used immediately, or placed in jars and frozen—a wonderful trick for those who find the idea of canning a little daunting. They can also be covered with oil and placed in the fridge. Chop up roasted tomatoes and add to soups, stews, eggs, or on a piece of rustic Italian bread.

INGREDIENTS
Tomatoes

Olive Oil

Salt

Dried herbs (rosemary, oregano, or thyme), optional

PROCEDURE
1. Preheat oven to 225°F (110°C).
2. Rinse and dry the tomatoes.
3. Cut the tomatoes in half around their middles.
4. Place on parchment-covered sheet pans with the cut side up. Drizzle lightly with olive oil and sprinkle some salt and optional herbs on top.
5. Place sheet pans in the preheated oven, and roast long and slow until they are shriveled-up and dry, about 3 hours—although, if your tomatoes are really big and juicy, it can take an hour or two longer. Set the timer to rotate the trays in the oven every 40 to 50 minutes so that they roast evenly.
6. Remove from the oven and cool.

Note To freeze, place roasted tomatoes in clean-lidded glass jars, leaving ½ inch (1 cm) of space at the top, and freeze for up to six months. Or store in the fridge: In clean-lidded glass jars, layer roasted tomatoes with garlic cloves and optional herbs, and pour olive oil over so all is covered. Close the lid, shake the jar gently, and place in the fridge for up to one month.

Panzanella Salad

For several years in a community garden I tended a small plot. I enjoyed taking part in the Friday night potlucks and Saturday compost socials. There were always salads picked fresh from the garden, big bowls of soup, and crusty Italian bread. If there was any bread left over, I was happy to take it home and make Panzanella, a salad made with sun-ripened tomatoes, cucumber, red onion, and fresh basil.

SERVES 4 TO 6

INGREDIENTS

¼ cup (60 ml) olive oil

6 cups day-old crusty Italian bread, such as ciabatta, sliced into 1-inch (2.5-cm) pieces

VINAIGRETTE

¼ cup (60 ml) good-quality balsamic vinegar, white wine vinegar, red wine vinegar, or rice wine vinegar

3 cloves garlic, minced or pressed

2 to 3 teaspoons Dijon mustard, depending on how strong you like it

½ teaspoon salt or seasoning salt (such as Spike)

⅛ teaspoon freshly ground black pepper

½ cup (120 ml) olive oil

SALAD

4 to 5 ripe tomatoes, chopped into bite-size pieces

1 cucumber, halved, seeded, and cut into bite-size pieces

1 red pepper, seeded and chopped into bite-size pieces

½ red onion, sliced thin

2 big handfuls fresh basil leaves (about 25 leaves), sliced into thin strips

1 cup (150 g) crumbled feta cheese (optional)

PROCEDURE

1. In a cast-iron skillet or sauté pan, heat the olive oil over medium-low heat. Add bread and cook for about 10 minutes, turning often until golden. Remove from pan and let drain on a paper towel.

2. Place the vinegar, garlic, mustard, salt, pepper, and olive oil in a lidded jar and shake well.

3. In a large bowl, place the tomatoes, cucumber, red pepper, red onion, basil, and optional feta. Toss lightly to mix.

4. Place the bread pieces in another bowl, pour the vinaigrette over them, and mix lightly. Add them to the salad, and toss well.

5. Let sit at room temperature for 30 minutes or up to 2 hours before serving.

Big Garden Salad with Garlic Lemon Dressing

Use whatever lettuce and greens you have on hand and add some chopped vegetables for good measure. Each time you make this salad, it can be different. Adjust the size of the salad—up for a crowd, or down for the solitary eater. The lemony dressing makes about one cup, and can be used for salads, as a dip for vegetables, over a bowl of brown rice and veggies, or drizzled on a baked potato. If you prefer vinaigrette, try Another Favorite Salad Dressing at the end of this recipe.

SALAD	Lettuce
	Baby kale leaves, red or green
	Spinach
	Arugula
	Mustard leaves and flowers
	Cabbage, shredded
	Carrots, grated
	Broccoli, small florets
	A few scallions, whites and greens, chopped
	Parmigiano-Reggiano cheese, grated (optional)
DRESSING	⅔ cup (160 ml) olive oil
	⅓ cup (75 ml) freshly squeezed lemon juice
	1 or more garlic cloves
	½ teaspoon Dijon mustard
	1½ teaspoons salt
	¼ teaspoon freshly ground black pepper

PROCEDURE

1. Wash all produce. Strip off the leaves of the kale from the stems. With your fingers, tear the lettuce, kale, spinach, and other leaves into bite-size pieces.
2. Place all salad ingredients in a large bowl and toss.
3. Place all dressing ingredients in the jar of a blender and blend thoroughly until smooth.
4. Add the dressing and optional cheese to the salad bowl and toss again.

Another Favorite Salad Dressing

I love to play around with balsamic, wine, rice, fruit, and citrus vinegars. This dressing is a fun way to experiment with them.

INGREDIENTS
- ¼ cup (60 ml) good-quality vinegar of your choice
- 3 cloves garlic, minced or pressed
- 2 to 3 teaspoons Dijon mustard, depending on how strong you like it
- ½ teaspoon salt or seasoning salt (such as Spike)
- ⅛ teaspoon freshly ground black pepper
- ½ cup (120 ml) olive oil

PROCEDURE
1. Place all ingredients in a lidded jar. Shake well.

Craft Vinegar Sometimes my travels take me to stores where I can sample craft vinegars. I buy small amounts and play with them in cooking and baking. Here are a few you can find on my pantry shelves:

Fig Balsamic
Pear Balsamic
Apple Balsamic
Raspberry Balsamic
Bragg's Apple Cider Vinegar
Cranberry Pear White Balsamic
Pomegranate Quince Balsamic
Orange Muscat Champagne Vinegar
Seasoned and Unseasoned Rice Wine Vinegar

Deep-Dish Ricotta Potluck Pie, page 162

Wood Stove Days

The Tree House

Tristan Jones once wrote that maintaining a boat "is like pouring seawater into a bottomless bucket." My bucket was the Tree House, a 1970s upscale hippie house on 10 acres of land. It had breathtaking territorial and water views as far as Mt. Baker near the Canadian border, 99 miles northeast of me as the crow flies. The house has the lifetime distinction of being the most unique and challenging place I have ever lived, and that is saying a lot, as there have been more than a few unique places I have called home. The house was suspended 35 feet up in the air on poles made from tall tree trunks, and except for a cedar boardwalk, no part of the house touched the ground. The architect's original plans even accommodated an eighty-year-old cedar tree growing through the ceiling.

I had outgrown the garden space at the post-and-beam house that wuzband #2 and I built, so we decided to look for more land where we could have a horse for compost, a cow for milk, a goat for cheese, chickens for eggs, fruit trees, berries, and a year-round garden, plus an already finished home. I was still deep in my dream of self-sufficient homesteading. By any wild stretch of the imagination, the Tree House did not fit the bill, but my wuzband loved it so much, my resolve wavered. "You won't recognize the place when I'm through restoring it," he said. I ignored the nagging feeling in my gut, took a deep breath, and signed on the dotted line.

In retrospect, that nagging feeling was a big caution sign flashing right in front of me. I had no idea that just a few months later, his life path would take him in a different direction than the one we were traveling together. Four months after we moved in, he announced that he needed to find himself, and he left to do so. Once again, I was a single mom, now with a nine-year-old boy, and the sole owner of a very expensive, uninsulated, tarpaper-and-shingle fixer, perched on a tree-covered mountainside. As for any repairs that might be needed, my wuzband left me with a hammer, a few screwdrivers, and a pipe wrench. I knew my way around a kitchen, but replacing rotting boards in a deck 35 feet up in the air, my first challenge in extreme rural living, was simply not in my skill set.

During the years I owned the house, I poured every available cent I had into it. I learned about wells, pressure tanks, skylights that failed due to the weight of heavy wet snow, and what was involved in rebuilding a logging road driveway that required four-wheel drive to navigate fair or foul weather. I was on a first-name basis with the phone repairman, who weekly patched the mile-long cable that lay above ground where the deer could snag it. I learned how to get rid of uninvited bats, packrats, and shrews who cohabited with us. The steady dribble of rocks and dirt coming down behind the house was a constant reminder that whoever had decided to build on this mountainside should have had their head examined.

After a year of challenges, I put the property up for sale and jumped at the chance to move off the mountain to help out on a blueberry u-pick farm 5 miles west. I returned regularly to check on the house and land, but what I needed was a reliable live-in caretaker, preferably with tools and skills, to live in the little guesthouse that shared the deck with the main house. I'm a very trusting person, but I think you will agree that, simply put, I was a fool when I agreed to let someone I had met only once take on that role.

We were first introduced at a Thanksgiving potluck. Kids, dogs, friends, and tables groaning with the weight of platters of delicious home-made food. When it was time to eat, we made a circle and joined hands while a newcomer gave the blessing. "Nice guy," I thought. "He seems to be a real holy man."

Later in the afternoon, when our bellies were full of salmon and slices of wild blackberry pie, we were introduced. He needed a place to live and, with a friend's nod of approval, I agreed to let him stay in the guesthouse. In lieu of rent, he would keep an eye on the property and do needed repairs and maintenance. A few days later, he moved in. It seemed almost too good to be true.

All seemed well at the start. It was okay with me that he had occasional friends over, and it was okay with him that I visited the house each week to dust, refresh the flowers, and make sure there were no sprung mousetraps that he might have missed. After a while, maintenance projects remained half done or not done at all. He assured me that he would finish everything up, it was just that he had been so busy playing music, reading, and contemplating the peaceful view. Ever the Pollyanna optimist, I brushed my frustration aside, and told him I knew he would get it done soon.

One week when I came to check on things, I heard what sounded like the heater fan on high in the guesthouse. It seemed odd since the weather had been sunny and warm. I was paying the utility bill and decided to investigate. "Hello? Anybody home?" I knocked on the door and went inside.

My ears led me up the narrow stairs to the closet in the guesthouse loft bedroom. I opened the door and found fans that were part of my caretaker's pot-growing operation. If it were reported by a potential buyer or real estate agent, I was in danger of losing the only asset I had. To say I was hopping mad is an understatement. Fortunately, the phone was working that day. I called everyone I could think of who might be able to help me locate this man I had believed to be so trustworthy. Then I waited. He showed up a few hours later, and I made it very clear that he was to move out immediately, as in right NOW. He said he was "a little busy" and asked for a few days grace. This was *not* the right reply. I countered with, "Move your blankity-blank stuff out today, or I will clear it out for you, and donate it to the charity of your choice." In less than an hour he was gone, and Duncan and I moved back from the farm.

At the end of our driveway were bundles of valuable old growth cedar shakes, stacked and covered with a tarp. They were extras from the post-and-beam house my wuzband and I had built together. One afternoon, I saw that the shape of the tarp didn't look quite right to my eye. I walked down to take a closer look. When I lifted the tarp, I saw that half the bundles were missing, and cardboard boxes were piled high in their place.

I placed a call to the sheriff and a deputy was sent. He looked at the pile and asked if there was anything else missing. We went to check on my two sea kayaks stored on pulleys underneath the deck. Yup. They were gone, too. The deputy asked me for as many details as possible, said it was hard luck about the loss, but told me that unless I knew where everything had been taken, or by whom, he couldn't do much of anything at all. He left me a card with his number and instructions to call if I found out anything.

The community here is small enough that it didn't take too long before I got a tip that a tiny off-the-grid cabin was being built not far away, and that I might find my cedar shakes there. I called the number on the card, and set up a time for two deputies to meet me at that location. When we arrived, there was a tiny cabin in the process of being sided with old-growth shakes. The deputies saw that they perfectly matched the ones I had brought with me for comparison. They told me to look around in case I saw anything else of mine that might have been taken.

As I walked the land to search, a young couple showed up. I recognized the man as one of my caretaker's friends whom I had seen at the Tree House. He saw me, smiled, and said hello. Somehow I kept my composure and returned the greeting, quickly steering the conversation to the little cabin under construction. He picked up the bait and said that our mutual friend was building it. Just then the deputies walked out through some trees and asked what they knew about the shakes. They spilled the beans. Yes, they had been taken. Yes, they were mine, but they had not taken them. Our mutual friend, the man I had thought to be so holy, had. I asked how anyone could possibly think it was okay to take another's possessions. "Holy Man's" friend patronizingly put his hand on my shoulder and said, "You had so much and we so little, we thought we should redistribute the wealth."

Now I really started to lose it, and in an increasingly agitated voice said, "Don't you dare touch me!" These were exactly the words the deputies needed to grab the hands of the couple, place them face down on the ground, and cuff them. Not exactly what I had in mind, as all I really wanted was to get my shakes and kayaks back. The girlfriend was crying now, but when she started to say something about the kayaks, her young man jabbed her with his elbow before she could finish. "We have no idea where our friend is," he said, "but if we see him, we'll let him know you are looking for him." The deputies

made it very clear that they would be looking for him, too.

To his credit, "Holy Man" did get in touch with me. He confessed to taking the shingles and paid me for them, but said he knew nothing about the kayaks. Although I never saw those boats again, for a few years, my eyes would scan for two forest green kayaks cradled on top of passing cars and trucks. I pictured the screaming u-turn I would make, how I would follow until the driver stopped and demand my boats back. Until one day, when a wise friend told me that I would be better off not thinking of the boats as mine anymore, because no matter how they were gotten, the kayaks now belonged to someone else. So I let them go, but not without adding a special blessing on those who had taken them.

May no harm come to those who
paddle these boats, but on each and
every long open water crossing, if
the paddlers experience very bad
tummy aches . . . that would be fine
by me.

My long-time friends and I laugh at the memory of what a crazy time that was at our potlucks, which are still going on over thirty years later. Just about all of these savory pies, stews, and soups have been enjoyed at least once, if not more, at them.

Deep-Dish Ricotta Potluck Pie

This pizza is really a homemade focaccia with plenty of toppings. When making the dough, you can tell if your yeast is active when the "yeasty beasties" start to bubble. If there is no bubbling, or it is very slow, the water may have been too hot, or your yeast may no longer be active, and needs to be replaced.

SERVES 6

DOUGH

2 tablespoons dry active yeast

1½ cups (350 ml) warm water

1 tablespoon granulated sugar

¼ cup (60 ml) olive oil

2 teaspoons salt

5 cups (726 g) unbleached all-purpose flour (you may not need all of it)

FILLING

2 cups (450 g) ricotta cheese

2 cups (200 g) grated Parmigiano-Reggiano cheese

1 bunch fresh spinach, washed, dried, and chopped

6 cloves garlic, minced

⅔ teaspoon salt

Freshly ground black pepper

TOPPING

2 cups (130 g) sliced mushrooms

1 cup (115 g) grated mozzarella cheese

1 large tomato, chopped, or ⅓ cup chopped roasted tomatoes (see page 150)

¼ cup (60 g) chopped marinated red pepper (optional)

1 teaspoon dried basil

1 teaspoon dried oregano

Olive oil, for brushing and drizzling

1. In a large bowl, place the yeast, warm water, and sugar. Mix lightly. Let sit for 5 minutes. You will see it bubbling if the yeast is active.

2. Stir in the oil and salt. Mix in 3½ cups (500 g) flour a little at a time.

3. When all the flour has been mixed in, turn the dough onto a lightly floured board. Sprinkle over 1 cup flour and knead for about 5 to 10 minutes. If you can add in the last ½ cup, that's great. If not, that's fine, too.

4. Put the dough in an oiled bowl. Cover and set in a warm spot. Let the dough rise for about 1 hour or until it has doubled in size. Punch down the dough with your fist.

5. Grease a 9-by-13-inch (23-by-33-cm) baking pan with some olive oil. Roll out the dough and press it into the pan. Be sure to press the dough all the way out to the edges of the pan.

6. Cover and set in a warm spot and let rise again for 20 to 30 minutes. Once dough is ready, preheat oven to 450°F (230°C).

7. Push down with your fingertips to make little divots all over the top of the dough. Brush with olive oil.

8. Place in preheated oven and immediately turn down to 375°F (190°C). Bake for 25 minutes.

9. To make the filling, place the ricotta, Parmigiano-Reggiano, spinach, garlic, salt, and pepper in a medium-size bowl and mix well. Set aside.

10. Remove the baked dough from oven. Brush with olive oil, and spread the filling evenly over the top.

11. For the topping, evenly layer the mushrooms, mozzarella, tomato, and optional red peppers on top of the filling. Sprinkle with basil and oregano, and drizzle more olive oil over the top.

12. Bake 20 to 25 minutes more until the cheese is bubbly.

Winter Vegetable Shepherd's Pie, page 166

Winter Vegetable Shepherd's Pie

While wuzband #2 and I built our post-and-beam dream home, the little one-room cabin in which we lived with two young children seemed straight out of a pioneering storybook. On one winter weekend, when the snow was nearly as deep as my two-year-old son was tall, our across-the-fence neighbors invited us over for a snowy supper potluck. While Duncan and his dad shoveled snow to make a path to their house, I peeled and chopped vegetables for this savory pie. When it was time for supper, we bundled up in boots, jackets, hats, and mittens, and carried a savory pie still warm from the oven to their door. The winter vegetables in this pie are flexible, so use others that you might have on hand, like turnip or rutabaga. That way you won't have to head out to the store on a snowy day.

SERVES 6 TO 8

INGREDIENTS

4 tablespoons (60 g) butter, plus additional ⅓ cup (75 g) for the potatoes

3 tablespoons (45 ml) olive oil

1 medium onion, cut into ½-inch (1-cm) chunks

1 teaspoon parsley

1 teaspoon thyme

½ teaspoon marjoram

1 bay leaf

1¾ teaspoons salt

½ cup (120 ml) apple or pear cider

2 tablespoons unbleached all-purpose flour (gluten-free flour can be substituted if desired)

2 cups (500 ml) stock (mushroom, chicken, or vegetable)

½ pound (225 g) mushrooms, cut in half

½ pound (225 g) boiling onions, brown skins removed, cut into halves, or 1 medium onion cut into 1- and ½-inch (4-cm) pieces

4 cloves garlic, chopped

4 medium carrots, peeled, cut in half, and cut into 2-inch (5-cm) half-moon pieces

2 large or 4 medium parsnips, peeled, cut in half, and cut into 2- to 3-inch (5- to 7-cm) half-moon pieces

Freshly ground black pepper

2¼ pounds (1 kg) potatoes, peeled and quartered

1 cup (110 g) grated sharp cheddar cheese (reserve ⅓ cup to sprinkle over the top)

½ teaspoon thyme

1. Melt 2 tablespoons butter and 1 tablespoon oil in a saucepan over medium heat. Add onion, parsley, thyme, marjoram, bay leaf, and ½ teaspoon salt, and cook until the onions are brown but not burned. Stir occasionally.

2. Add the cider and cook until the liquid is reduced by half. Add flour and stock. Stir with a spoon to break up any lumps. Bring to a boil, turn down heat, and simmer for about 5 minutes while stirring occasionally. Set the sauce aside.

3. Melt 1 tablespoon butter and 1 tablespoon oil in a large skillet over medium heat. Add the mushrooms and ¼ teaspoon salt, turn the heat to high, and cook for 3 minutes while stirring often. Remove from heat, turn the mushrooms into a bowl, and set aside.

4. Melt another 1 tablespoon butter and 1 tablespoon oil in the skillet over medium-high heat. Add boiling onions, garlic, carrots, and parsnips, and cook for 5 minutes, stirring occasionally. Add the mushrooms and half the sauce, cover pan, lower heat, and simmer for 5 minutes, stirring occasionally.

5. Add the remaining sauce. Raise the heat to medium and cook for 5 minutes, stirring occasionally. Add salt and pepper to taste.

6. Place potatoes in a saucepan and cover with about 2 inches (5 cm) of water. Add 1 teaspoon salt, and boil for about 15 minutes until tender. Drain off the water.

7. Put the potatoes back into the pot, with ⅓ cup butter (75 g), ⅔ cup cheese, and thyme, and mash until smooth. A few lumps are okay. Add salt and pepper to your taste.

8. Remove the bay leaf from the filling and turn into an 8-by-12-inch (20-by-30-cm) baking pan. Evenly spread the potato mixture over the filling. Sprinkle the remaining cheese over the top.

9. When ready to bake, preheat the oven to 375°F (190°C) and bake for 35 to 40 minutes.

Note If you have any leftover Brussels sprouts from Thanksgiving dinner, pop them into the filling, too (see Brussels, Bacon, and Blue, page 139).

Playgroup Casserole

Playgroup was the day we most looked forward to when Duncan was little. It wasn't long before multi-family potlucks were added to our calendar. This very easy casserole, from one of our potlucks, will be enjoyed by folks both big and little.

SERVES 6 TO 8

INGREDIENTS

½ cup (115 ml) melted butter, plus more for greasing the baking dish

One 14.75-ounce (418-g) can cream-style corn

One 4-ounce (113-g) can diced green chilies

One 2-ounce (57-g) jar pimentos, drained

2 large eggs, beaten

½ cup (60 g) cornmeal

½ teaspoon salt

1 cup (225 g) sour cream

2 cups (230 g) grated jack cheese

PROCEDURE

1. Preheat oven to 375°F (190°C).
2. Butter a shallow 1½-quart baking dish.
3. Combine all ingredients in a big bowl and mix until combined.
4. Pour ingredients into the baking dish.
5. Bake uncovered for 40 minutes.

Falling Down on the Job

Early one morning, I packed up my pies and supplies, and drove to Seattle, a three-hour journey for me, to do a pie-making demonstration. Driving and parking can be challenging in big cities, so I factored in extra time, keyed the address of the demonstration location into my phone's GPS, made sure I had water and snacks if I got delayed, and hit the road.

I had whistled for The Parking Fairy the night before I left with hopes that she might bestow a bit of asphalt grace my way. Downtown Seattle? On a rainy Friday afternoon? At rush hour? Sure, no problem. Fortunately, she heard me and came through with a spot where I could double park just outside the location for a few moments to bring in my rolling cooler and baskets. I turned on my flashers, opened the hatch, got out my gear, and, pulling the cooler with my right hand and carrying a pie basket with my left, got within feet of the door when my feet went out from under me. Down went the cooler. Down went the pie basket. Down went me. I landed on my hip. Owie! I bent my wrist back. Double owie! The lid of the cooler opened and berries were rolling around on the street. Oh no! I was hurt but immediately kicked into crisis mode . . . you know, the one where you push pain aside and keep going.

A hand up would have been nice. An "Are you all right?" would have been appreciated. A "Do you need help?" would have been best of all. I looked up and said, "I'm hurt." Not one person on the street around me stopped. NOT ONE! I fell down on the job, but I feel that others, who saw what happened, did too. They glanced and kept on walking, too busy or preoccupied with phone texting to help.

I got to my knees, corralled the rolling fruit, checked that the pies were still okay, slowly got up, and dropped off my demonstration gear at my destination. Then I headed back out to my car to get it to a parking garage. At the other end of the very long day, I thought about what had happened, and how lucky I had been to walk away with only a big bruise on my hip, some sore ribs, and a stiff neck. I also thought of the bigger hurt I felt on the inside, of how invisible, abandoned, and frustrated I felt that no one had stopped to help me when I said I was hurt. We seem to have forgotten how important it is to help others no matter what.

So, here are a few things to think about. Walk carefully when it is slippery and wet, and please take a moment to lend a hand and show some care. You never know who may need it.

Snowy Day Lentil Soup

This soup is very comforting after a long snowy slog up a mountainside. It can be made with green lentils, but the combination of red and green makes a nice texture. Top off each bowl with a little Parmigiano-Reggiano cheese. It's a little pricier than other Parmesan cheeses, but it is used mainly as a condiment, so a little goes a long way.

SERVES 8 TO 10 WITH LEFTOVERS

INGREDIENTS

¼ cup (60 ml) olive oil

1½ yellow onions, chopped

4 medium carrots, peeled and chopped

2 medium sweet potatoes, peeled and chopped

3 stalks of celery, chopped

5 cloves garlic (optional)

1 teaspoon salt

½ teaspoon marjoram

1 teaspoon oregano

1 teaspoon basil

⅛ teaspoon red pepper flakes

1 cup (190 g) green lentils

1 cup (210 g) red lentils

10 cups (2.4 l) chicken stock or water

½ to ¾ cup (50 to 75 g) grated Parmigiano-Reggiano cheese or sharp cheese of your choice, for serving

PROCEDURE

1. In a large Dutch oven, warm the olive oil over medium heat. Add all the chopped vegetables and salt, and cook for about 10 minutes. Stir occasionally.
2. Add the marjoram, oregano, basil, and red pepper flakes, and stir briefly.
3. Add the lentils and broth or water, and stir. Turn the heat up until you see some steady vigorous bubbling in the pot. Then turn the heat to low, cover, and simmer for about 40 minutes. You can cook longer if you wish, but not so long that everything gets mushy.
4. Taste and add more salt if needed.
5. Serve in individual bowls with grated cheese sprinkled on top.

Hearty Cheddar and Potato Soup

Each fall at Pie Cottage, we have an apple cider pressing and potluck with friends and family. One record year we pressed ninety gallons. For the potluck, I always make a triple batch of this soup, and bake up some corn bread (see page 181). When the soup is ready, I carry the big steaming pot outside and set it on the makeshift table—two sawhorses with a door on the top. Even if you aren't going to a cider pressing, this soup is perfect on a crisp, fall day.

SERVES 6

INGREDIENTS

4 cups (1 l) water or chicken stock

4 medium red or Yellow Finn unpeeled potatoes, diced

2 medium onions, chopped

2 stalks celery, sliced in ¼-inch (5-mm) half moons

1½ teaspoons salt

¼ cup (60 g) butter

2 tablespoons unbleached all-purpose flour or gluten-free flour

2 cups (475 ml) milk

⅛ teaspoon salt

¾ teaspoon dry mustard

2 cups (230 g) grated sharp cheddar cheese

¼ cup minced parsley

PROCEDURE

1. Place water or stock in a large pot and bring to a boil. Add potatoes, onions, celery, and salt. Turn heat to medium, cover, and cook for 15 minutes.
2. Melt butter in a medium saucepan over low heat. Stir in the flour. Slowly pour in the milk and stir while heating. Whisk in the salt and mustard. Add the cheese and let it melt.
3. Pour the milk and cheese mixture into the large pot with the cooked vegetables. Add the parsley. Simmer uncovered over low heat for about 15 minutes. Stir often to make sure it isn't sticking or burning on the bottom.

Note Kerrygold Aged Cheddar with Irish Whiskey Cheese is very tasty grated on top.

White Bean Soup

When the weather turns chilly, this hearty soup is the one I turn to. It is excellent with corn bread hot out of the oven (see page 181). I have served it at Pie Camps at Pie Cottage, where I'm always asked if I might please share the recipe. To make this bean soup, it takes just three easy steps: 1. Cook the beans. 2. Chop and sauté the vegetables. 3. Combine the beans and veggies, and simmer until done.

SERVES 8 TO 10

INGREDIENTS

2 cups (370 g) dry white beans

3 quarts (2.8 l) water or stock (chicken or vegetable), or a combination of water and stock

1 bay leaf (optional)

5 medium potatoes (red or yellow)

4 medium carrots

4 stalks celery

2 medium yellow onions

3 tablespoons (45 g) olive oil, plus more for serving

6 cloves garlic, minced

1 tablespoon chopped fresh rosemary

1 tablespoon fresh thyme

2 teaspoons salt

Parmigiano-Reggiano cheese (optional)

Pesto (see page 149) (optional)

8 ounces pasta, cooked al dente (optional)

CONTINUED

1. Rinse dry beans several times, place them in a Dutch oven or lidded pot, cover with a few inches of water, and bring to a boil for 3 minutes. Remove and discard any foam on top. Let sit for 1 hour.
2. Rinse the beans, and cover them again with 3 quarts (2.8 l) fresh water, stock, or a combination of water and stock. Bring the beans to a boil for about 3 minutes. Remove and discard any foam on top. Turn down the heat, add the optional bay leaf, and simmer partially covered for about 30 minutes while you chop the vegetables.
3. Chop the potatoes, carrots, celery, and onions so that they are all about ½ to ¾ inches (1 to 2 cm) in size. You can use a food processor on the pulse setting if you'd like.
4. Heat a large cast-iron frying pan over medium heat and add the olive oil. Add the potatoes, carrots, celery, and onions and let cook for about 6 minutes, stirring occasionally.
5. Add the garlic to the vegetables along with the rosemary, thyme, and salt. Let cook for another 3 to 4 minutes, stirring occasionally.
6. Add the entire vegetable mixture to the soup pot and continue simmering for another 30 minutes or until the beans are soft.
7. Add the pasta, if using, towards the end of the simmer.
8. Taste and add salt if needed. Serve with a little olive oil drizzled and some freshly grated Parmigiano-Reggiano cheese or a dollop of pesto.

Note For a really big crowd, add any sort of pasta cooked al dente, with a little extra liquid if needed.

Food Processor or Knife?

I received my first food processor, a 1979 Cuisinart DLC-7, in 1979. Nearly forty years later, it still runs like a champ. I think of it as an old friend and use it when preparing large batches of onions, carrots, and celery for soups and dips. In order to ensure that small pieces of onion are still visible instead of turning into puree, I've gotten very good at lightly touching the pulse bar as if it were a hot potato. The blade doesn't go around so frantically fast that way.

I love the convenience of the processor, but I'm never thrilled about having to wash up its bowl, blade, and lid, in addition to a knife and cutting board. When only one carrot or half an onion is needed, a sharp knife and cutting board—the most oft used tools in my kitchen—are much easier. I find mindful and careful chopping to be a meditation. Whether by hand or by food processor, it's a matter of choice, time, and what you enjoy doing the most.

When using a food processor, ingredients such as onions will need to be peeled and cut to a size that a food processor can handle. After the machine has processed it to the size called for in the recipe, use a rubber spatula to get all the little bits and pieces scraped out. Then rinse it well, and do a quick dry with a towel, before starting on the next ingredient to be chopped.

A sharp knife is a safer knife because it will slice and chop ingredients more easily than dull ones that might bounce off a sturdy onion, parsnip, beet, or potato. Be sure to curl the fingertips of the hand that is holding the ingredient to avoid nicking them . . . or worse.

Three Ways to Cook Beans

There's no getting around the fact that cooking dry beans takes time. It's an easy process, and I love the aroma of beans simmering with herbs and spices. I used to soak dry beans overnight before cooking them, but over the years found that I get the same results by bringing the beans to a boil for a few minutes, letting them sit for an hour, and then cooking. And lest you think that you can't make a recipe at the last minute if you've forgotten to soak and cook them, canned beans are just the ticket.

If dry beans won't soften after a long cook, most likely it is because they are old and stale. Whether buying in bags or from the bulk bin, buy from a store that has a good turnover of products to ensure that the beans are fresh.

Either way you do it, beans will soak up quite a bit of water while cooking, so do check in on them regularly to see if you need to add more. I add hot boiling water from my tea kettle to keep the beans at a steady cooking temperature.

The Long Way

Rinse dry beans several times, place them in a Dutch oven or large lidded pot, cover with a few inches of water, and soak overnight or at least 3 hours. Rinse the beans, and cover them again with fresh water. Bring the beans to a boil for 2 to 3 minutes. Remove and discard any foam on top. Turn down the heat to low, cover, and simmer. Add any seasonings called for in a recipe, and continue to simmer until the beans are soft, for a total of 1 to 3 hours. Check every half hour or so and add extra water as needed. Older beans will take longer.

The Medium Way

Rinse dry beans several times, place them in a Dutch oven or large lidded pot, cover with a few inches of water, and bring to a boil for 3 minutes. Remove and discard any foam on top. Let sit for 1 hour. Bring the beans back to a boil, turn the heat down to low, cover, and simmer. Add any seasonings called for in a recipe, and continue to cook until the beans are tender, about 60 to 90 minutes total. Check every half hour or so and add extra boiling water as needed. Garbanzo beans will take about twice as long to cook. Older beans will also take longer.

The Short Way

Get out the can opener and use canned beans.

Stone Soup

Do you remember the story "Stone Soup"? It's the tale where hungry soldiers convince villagers to share a small amount of food to make a meal. They fill the pot, cook the soup, and a celebration follows. The soup is an easy one to bring to life, and it was often shared at an urban community garden where I used to tend a plot. The recipe begs for variation, so use whatever is fresh at your farmers' market, in the produce aisle at the local grocery, or pulled right from the garden beds outside the kitchen door. Serve with thick slices of hearty rustic Italian bread to mop up any of the thick broth that might be left in the bowl. Any way you make it, you'll have a satisfying bowlful of flavor to share. If you want to soak your beans overnight before cooking, be sure to take a look at Three Ways to Cook Beans on page 177. Using canned beans is always an option, too.

MAKES ABOUT 3 QUARTS

INGREDIENTS

½ pound (about 200 g) dry red or white beans, such as kidney, Northern white, or cannellini, or two 15-ounce cans (850 g total) beans

2 tablespoons (30 ml) olive oil, plus more for serving

5 to 7 cloves garlic, minced

1 tablespoon chopped fresh rosemary

1½ teaspoons chopped fresh oregano

2 large tomatoes, cored and coarsely chopped

1 small (about 1 to 1½ lbs or 450 to 675 g) winter squash, peeled and coarsely chopped

2 to 3 carrots, peeled and coarsely chopped into half moons or other shapes of your choice

2 quarts (2 l) water or chicken stock

1 bunch kale, coarsely chopped

1 to 2 cups (130 to 260 g) fresh or frozen peas

1 cup (90 g) elbow macaroni or other small tube-shaped pasta

Salt and freshly ground black pepper

1 handful fresh parsley, chopped

½ cup (50 g) grated Parmigiano-Reggiano cheese (optional)

CONTINUED

1. Rinse dry beans several times, place them in a Dutch oven or lidded pot, cover with a few inches of water, and bring to a boil for 3 minutes. Remove and discard any foam on top. Let sit for 1 hour.

2. Rinse the beans, cover them again with fresh water, and bring to a boil for 3 minutes. Remove and discard any foam on top. Turn down the heat, cover, and simmer for about 90 minutes or until the beans are tender. Older beans will take longer. Drain the beans and set aside. If using canned beans, you can skip this step.

3. Dry out the bottom of a Dutch oven or large pot, and heat olive oil over medium heat. Add garlic and sauté for 30 to 60 seconds. Add the rosemary, oregano, tomatoes, squash, and carrots and sauté for 3 or 4 minutes.

4. Put the cooked or canned beans back in the pot and cover with about 2 quarts (2 liters) water or stock. Bring to a boil, turn the heat down, partially cover, and simmer for at least 30 minutes, stirring occasionally.

5. Add coarsely chopped kale, peas, and pasta. Continue cooking until the pasta is tender. Season with salt and pepper to taste.

6. Serve with extra olive oil to drizzle on top, chopped parsley, and optional Parmigiano-Reggiano.

Note Leftover Roasted Root Vegetables (see page 120) add a lot of flavor to this soup. When using dried herbs, I use half the amount of fresh.

Kate's Corn Bread, Gluten-Free or Gluten-Full

Everyone likes corn bread, especially when it is hot out of the oven and served with a pat of melting butter on top. This is a slightly moist version that doesn't dry out overnight when covered. I've been known to pour warm milk and maple syrup over a leftover slice for breakfast. The only difference between the gluten-free and the gluten-full version is which flour you use. It's great with either one. My son Duncan likes corn bread a bit sweeter than I do. If you do as well, feel free to add a tablespoon or two more sugar.

SERVES 4 TO 6

INGREDIENTS

1 cup (120 g) cornmeal (use gluten-free cornmeal if desired)

1 cup (146 g) unbleached all-purpose flour or 1 cup (158 g) all-purpose gluten-free flour

¼ cup (50 g) granulated sugar

1 teaspoon baking soda

2 teaspoons cream of tartar

¾ teaspoon salt

1 cup (225 g) sour cream or plain unsweetened yogurt

¼ cup (60 ml) milk, half and half, or even whipping cream

2 large eggs, fork beaten

¼ cup (60 ml) butter, melted

PROCEDURE

1. Preheat the oven to 425°F (220°C).
2. Butter a square 9-inch (23-cm) baking dish, or something close to that size.
3. Place the cornmeal, flour, sugar, baking soda, cream of tartar, and salt into a medium-size bowl, and mix to combine.
4. In a larger bowl, mix together the sour cream or yogurt. Add the milk, half and half, or whipped cream. Add the fork beaten eggs and melted butter. Mix everything together until blended.
5. Pour the dry ingredients into the wet, and mix until everything is moistened, and just comes together.
6. Fold into the greased baking dish and bake in the preheated oven for about 20 minutes.
7. Let cool a bit, and cut into whatever size you deem fit for a serving.

Black Bean Chili, page 184

Kate's Corn Bread, page 181

Black Bean Chili

I've been making Black Bean Chili in many variations for family and friends for decades. This recipe freezes beautifully so you can always have some "fast food" when you need it. Some things get better with age, and this chili tastes even better on the second day. I like it best made with dry beans that I soak and cook, but it's fast and easy to make with canned beans, too. For red bean chili, red kidney beans may be substituted.

SERVES 6

INGREDIENTS

2 cups dry black beans or four15-ounce (425-g) cans black beans

6 cups (1.4 l) water

One 14.5-ounce (411-g) can diced tomatoes or up to 1 cup chopped oven-roasted tomatoes (see page 150)

2 to 3 bay leaves

2 to 3 tablespoons (30 to 45 ml) olive oil

3 to 4 medium onions, chopped

6 cloves garlic, minced

2 medium carrots, chopped

1 to 2 tablespoons mild chili powder

2 teaspoons salt

½ teaspoon smoked paprika (optional)

⅛ to ¼ teaspoon cayenne (optional)

Extra minced onion, for serving

Grated cheddar cheese, for serving

Sour cream, for serving

1. Rinse dry beans several times, place them in a Dutch oven or lidded pot, cover with a few inches of water, and bring to a boil for 3 minutes. Remove and discard any foam on top. Let sit for 1 hour.
2. Rinse the beans and cover them again with fresh water. Bring the beans to a boil for 2 to 3 minutes. Turn down the heat. Cover and simmer until soft, about 1 hour. Add extra water as needed. Skim off and discard any foam that rises to the top.
3. Add the tomatoes and bay leaves, and simmer covered for another 30 minutes.
4. In a large cast-iron skillet or frying pan, heat the olive oil, and sauté onions, garlic, and carrots and cook until the onions are soft and starting to brown. Stir in the chili powder, salt, and optional smoked paprika and cayenne. Cook for 2 to 3 minutes more while stirring occasionally, and then add to the beans.
5. Simmer for 20 to 30 minutes more uncovered. Stir occasionally. Add more liquid if needed. Add more salt to your taste.
6. Serve with minced onion, grated cheese, and sour cream.

Making Sense of It All

Food has . . .

The sense of sight: color, amount, arrangement

The sense of texture: soft, hard, mushy, crunchy, smooth, lumpy

The sense of smell: fragrant, fruity, citrus, woody and resinous, chemical, sweet, minty, toasted, nutty, pungent, and sometimes decayed

The sense of sound: munch, crunch, slurp

The sense of taste: salty, sour, sweet, bitter

Minestrone for All Seasons

I like the ease and flexibility of minestrone because the ingredients can change seasonally using what is ready to be harvested from the garden or the farmers' market. In the spring, that could be spinach, asparagus, and peas; in summer, green beans and zucchini; and during fall and winter, squash, chard, and kale. My can opener comes in handy for whichever color beans—red, white, or black—are on my shelf. Make enough for leftovers since the flavors are even better on the second day.

MAKES 6 GENEROUS SERVINGS

INGREDIENTS

2 tablespoons (30 ml) olive oil

5 scallions, whites and greens, sliced

3 to 4 large cloves garlic, minced

1 to 2 medium carrots, chopped

3 to 4 red or yellow potatoes, cut into 1-inch (2.5-cm) pieces

One 15-ounce (425-g) can diced tomatoes

4 cups (1 l) chicken stock

¼ cup (60 ml) dry red wine

1 teaspoon salt

One 15.5-ounce (439-g) can red, white, or black beans, rinsed and drained

½ pound (230 g) asparagus or green beans, cut into 1-inch (2.5-cm) pieces

1 bunch greens (chard, spinach, or kale), cut into thin strips

¼ cup (60 ml) pesto, either homemade (see page 149) or store-bought

½ teaspoon freshly ground black pepper

Grated Parmigiano-Reggiano cheese, for serving

PROCEDURE

1. Heat the oil in a large heavy pot over medium-low heat. Add the scallions and garlic, and sauté for 1 minute. Raise the heat to medium, add the carrots and potatoes, and cook for another 2 minutes while you stir everything around a bit.
2. Add the diced tomatoes, chicken stock, wine, and salt. Bring up to a boil, and immediately turn down to simmer. Cover and let cook for 10 to 15 minutes.
3. Add the white, red, or black beans, and cook for 5 minutes more.
4. Add the asparagus or green beans, and cook for 2 more minutes.
5. Add the greens. Stir and cook for another minute or two.
6. Add the pesto and pepper. Taste, and add more salt if you like.
7. Serve with grated Parmigiano-Reggiano cheese on top.

Wild Mushroom Soup with Grilled Garlic Toast

Wuzband #3 said, "Let's go mushrooming!," so on a crisp fall day, after a rain, we packed my VW Camper with mushroom baskets and picnic lunch, and headed off to one of his secret spots in the Cascade Mountains. After a mile or so of hiking, he led us off trail. There they were. More wild mushrooms than I had ever seen in one location. We picked until our baskets were full to the brim, and then carried our haul back to the camper. The beauty of a camper is that the kitchen can be anywhere you are, and this off-road spot was no exception. I pulled out a cutting board, knife, pot, and pan, tucked away for moments like these, and made mushroom soup. He made a small campfire, and grilled some garlic toast in a cast-iron skillet. And that secret spot? Well, in true 'shroomer tradition, it will have to remain a secret.

Wild chanterelle, lobster, and oyster mushrooms are lovely in this soup, but store-bought ones will do, too.

SERVES 4 TO 6

INGREDIENTS

¼ cup (60 ml) olive oil

1½ pounds (700 g) mushrooms, cleaned and roughly chopped

6 shallots, finely chopped

2 cloves garlic, chopped

½ cup (120 ml) white wine

A sprig of fresh thyme

4 cups (about 1 l) milk

Salt and freshly ground black pepper, to taste

PROCEDURE

1. In a large soup pot, heat the oil over medium low heat. Add mushrooms and shallots, and sauté for 5 minutes, stirring occasionally.
2. Add garlic and sauté a few minutes more. Give a stir every now and then.
3. Add the wine and stir. Cook for 2 to 3 minutes more.
4. Add thyme, milk, salt, and pepper, and stir. Cook for 3 or 4 minutes until heated through.
5. Put in a blender and pulse until it is relatively smooth but you can still see some small pieces of mushrooms. Return to the pot, and re-heat over low.
6. Serve with garlic toast (recipe follows).

Garlic Toast

No need for butter on this toast.

INGREDIENTS

Rustic Italian bread, such as Ciabatta, sliced

Olive oil

Several cloves garlic, peeled

Salt

PROCEDURE

1. Brush both sides of bread lightly with olive oil.
2. Toast the bread on both sides in a cast-iron frying pan, on a grill, or under a broiler. Remove with a spatula or tongs so you won't burn your fingers.
3. Take a garlic clove and rub it briskly and lightly over both sides of the toasted bread.
4. Sprinkle with a little salt.
5. Serve while still warm.

Wild Mushroom Soup with Grilled Garlic Toast, page 188

Hurry-Up Soup

We all have days when there is no time to make supper. This is exactly the kind of day when it's great to have a recipe that requires nothing more than a few cans from the pantry, a can opener, a pot, and spoon for stirring. This is a good soup to make when unexpected, hungry friends drop by, too.

SERVES 4 TO 6

INGREDIENTS

1 box (946 ml, about 4 cups) store-bought chicken, beef, or vegetable stock

Two 15-ounce cans (850 g total) beans (red, black, white, or a combination)

One 15-ounce (425-g) can tomato sauce

One 15-ounce (425-g) can diced tomatoes

One 15.5-ounce (439-g) can organic corn

Parmigiano-Reggiano cheese, grated (optional)

PROCEDURE

1. Open the box of stock and all the cans. Drain the liquid from the beans and corn and discard. Turn the ingredients into a medium to large saucepan.
2. Turn the heat to medium low. Stir occasionally.
3. When it is hot enough, serve with some optional grated Parmigiano Reggiano.

Note For a variation on the soup, you can add a can of green or red enchilada sauce.

Under-the-Weather Chicken Broth

Sipping on mugs of this healing broth throughout the day when I'm under the weather has helped to quickly move along many aches, pains, colds, and flu.

INGREDIENTS

4 cups (1 l) chicken broth, either homemade or store-bought

6 cloves garlic, chopped

¼ cup (40 g) grated fresh ginger

PROCEDURE

1. Place the stock in a medium-size pan and bring to a boil.
2. Add the garlic and ginger. Turn down the heat and let simmer for 5 to 10 minutes.
3. Set a small sieve strainer on top of a mug and ladle some of the broth into it. Put any solids back into the pot. Add more broth to the garlic and ginger as needed.

Crockpot Cooking In the 1970s, crockpots were the latest and greatest gadget on just about every kitchen counter, my mom's being no exception. The manual for her original avocado green Rival model said, "Cooks all day while the cook's away." Apparently it was trying to appeal to women who were leaving their aprons at home to join the workforce, but women working were nothing new in our household. My grandmother, my mom, and I all worked to support our families. As an Iowa farm girl preferring cast-iron, my grandmother was too old-school to have much of a fondness for the crockpot, but my mom did, and I find it to be a tool I use if I'm not going to be around to stir the soup, or check on the stew. I don't worry about browning the meat first, I just put all the ingredients for a recipe into the crockpot, turn it on, and don't give it another thought until I walk in the door to the delicious aroma of a supper that is all ready. Although there are new slow cookers on the market that do everything from browning meat, sautéing onions, baking cake, and pressure cooking, the one I have is a close kin to my mom's original model, and still seems like a bit of kitchen magic to me.

Chicken Soup

If you haven't made homemade chicken soup before, you are in for a treat. I think it's easily one of the best tastes of home. You'll need a big pot, a whole cut-up chicken, chopped vegetables, a little salt and pepper, and water to cover it all. While the soup simmers, give it an occasional taste. If you forget to put in the parsnips, like sometimes I do, it will still be delicious.

SERVES 8

INGREDIENTS

12 cups (3 l) water

3 carrots, peeled and chopped

1 large stalk celery, sliced in ½-inch (1-cm) half-moons

4 small parsnips, peeled and chopped

1 large onion, chopped

1 whole chicken, cut into pieces

1 tablespoon salt

¼ teaspoon freshly ground black pepper

PROCEDURE

1. In a big pot, add the water. Turn the heat to high and bring the water to a boil.
2. While waiting for the water to boil, chop the vegetables.
3. Add the chicken pieces, vegetables, salt, and pepper.
4. Lower the heat and simmer, covered, for 1 hour. Lift the chicken pieces from the pot and remove and discard the bones. Cut the meat into bite-size pieces and return to the pot.
5. You can simmer longer if you like, but it is fine to serve right away. Taste the broth and add more salt to your own taste.

Note You can cool the soup overnight and skim off the fat that rises to the top before reheating. For a thicker soup, place some of the broth and vegetables into a blender and puree. Return to the pot and add the cut chicken pieces. A spoonful of pesto with each serving is a delicious addition.

My Grandmother's Oven-Baked Beef Stew

My grandmother taught me to make beef stew when I was a girl. Now, when my cottage is scented with its aroma, it takes me right back to the time when I was helping to stir everything into her big cast-iron pot. Of course, the pot was way too heavy for me to lift by myself back then, so after she opened the oven door, and placed the stew inside, we carefully closed the door together.

SERVES 4 TO 6

INGREDIENTS

2 tablespoons unbleached all-purpose flour

¼ teaspoon paprika

¼ teaspoon salt

¼ teaspoon freshly ground black pepper

2 pounds (900 g) stew meat, cut into approximately 1½-inch (4-cm) cubes

3 tablespoons (45 ml) olive oil

1 medium onion, sliced thin

4 medium carrots, peeled and sliced into ½-inch (1-cm) moons

4 red potatoes, unpeeled and cubed in ½-inch (1-cm) pieces

2 stalks celery, chopped into ½-inch (1-cm) half moons

One 15-ounce (425-g) can tomato sauce

½ teaspoon dried rosemary or thyme

1 bay leaf

1½ cups (350 ml) beef stock or water

1 cup (130 g) frozen peas

CONTINUED

1. Preheat oven to 400°F (200°C).
2. Mix the flour, paprika, salt, and pepper together and place in a medium-size paper bag. Put in the meat cubes and shake well until all sides are coated.
3. In a 5-quart Dutch oven, heat the olive oil over medium heat, add seasoned meat, and brown on all sides.
4. Add the onion, carrots, potatoes, celery, tomato sauce, rosemary or thyme, bay leaf, and beef stock or water. Raise the heat and bring to a boil.
5. Remove from heat, and bake uncovered for 20 minutes at 400°F (200°C).
6. Lower the heat to 350°F (180°C), cover, and continue baking for 90 minutes more.
7. Remove from oven and stir in frozen peas. Let sit while you set the table so the peas can defrost. Stir before serving.

Meaty Thoughts

Three friends and I once bought a quarter of a cow from a hobby rancher, who raised beef sustainably before "sustainably" was even a thing. I didn't serve "meat and potatoes" on a daily basis, so I figured that my quarter of a quarter would last my family for most of one year. The cow went off to the butcher, and when I got the call to pick up our portion, I brought home boxes with packages neatly wrapped in white butcher paper and stamped, STEAK, ROAST, RIBS, STEW, HAMBURGER, and SOUP BONES. That quarter of a quarter filled about half of my chest freezer. Every once in a while it is a treat to cook up steaks or a roast, but it is the stew, hamburger, and soup bones that are the best fit for my cooking style, which is heavily influenced by my grandmother, who raised her children as a single mom in the Depression era. My grandmother taught me not only how to make beef stew, but also that long slow cooking of less expensive cuts is a great way to stretch a food budget.

Lamb Stew

This is a hearty lamb stew seasoned with herbs, tomatoes, and red wine. Buy a boneless leg of lamb if you like, and cube up your own stew meat.

SERVES 6 TO 8

INGREDIENTS

3 tablespoons (45 ml) olive oil

3 pounds (1.3 kg) lamb stew meat, cut into 1½-inch (4-cm) cubes

2 large onions, sliced thin

1 stalk celery, chopped into ½-inch (1-cm) half moons

3 medium carrots, peeled and sliced into ½-inch (1-cm) moons

One 15-ounce (425-g) can tomato sauce

2 tomatoes, chopped, or one 15.5-ounce (415-g) can diced tomatoes

2 cup (475 ml) chicken or beef stock

1 cup (250 ml) red wine

1 teaspoon granulated sugar

4 cloves garlic, minced

2 bay leaves

1½ teaspoons dried thyme

¼ teaspoon salt

¼ teaspoon freshly ground black pepper

1 cup (130 g) frozen peas

PROCEDURE

1. In a 5-quart Dutch oven, heat 2 tablespoons (30 ml) olive oil over medium heat, add one third of the lamb pieces, and brown on all sides. Remove, and set aside to drain. Repeat with other two batches, adding a bit more oil if needed.

2. Add remaining 1 tablespoon (15 ml) olive oil and onions to pan, and sauté for about 5 minutes until soft.

3. Add celery, carrots, tomato sauce, and tomatoes, turn heat to medium low, and cook for 5 to 7 minutes, stirring occasionally.

4. Pour off any excess fat and drippings from the meat, and return browned lamb pieces to the pan. Add stock, red wine, sugar, garlic, bay leaves, thyme, salt, and pepper. Raise the heat and bring to a boil. Cover the pot, and immediately turn the heat down to low, and simmer for 1½ hours. Stir occasionally, adding water or stock as needed.

5. Remove the bay leaf and add the peas. Return to a boil and cook for another few minutes. Add salt and pepper to taste.

How to Roast a Chicken, page 204

Suppertime

Growing a Life

ove to the country. Have a family. Build a home. Tend a garden. Grow a life. That was my dream and, for a time, it came true. The seed of the dream was planted on a camping trip to to the Olympic Peninsula where I unexpectedly met the man who, for a time, would help make it a reality. Our courtship was brief . . . a whirlwind twenty-eight days to be exact. We talked and then talked some more. I was overjoyed that he shared my dream. A self-taught woodworker, he had the skills, and, at that time, I had the means. Idealistic and in love, we took a flying leap of faith, married, and with my nearly six-year-old daughter, moved to a place both of us had been to only once.

Our first home was an old house on a retired dairy farm where we spent a year getting to know each other and our new community. We searched for the right spot to build our dream home and settled on 2½ beautiful acres in the foothills of the Olympic Mountains. It was partially treed and partially opened, had an already cleared homesite, a big shop building for him, a storage barn, water, septic, power, and the sweetest little cabin I had ever seen. We pared down our belongings to basics so the three of us, plus my growing belly now carrying our son, Duncan, could move in. On our first night in the cabin, I felt that I had stepped into Laura Ingalls Wilder's book *Little House in the Big Woods*.

Our days were defined by seasonal tasks: tending the garden, putting up food, bringing in enough cord wood to keep the wood stove fed through the cold season, at night snuggling on the couch reading books and listening to music, and building our homestead during the day. Duncan was born on a snowy winter's night in the loft, while strains of The Beatles' song "In My Life" played softly in the background. We were snug, together, and blissfully happy.

My wuzband had predicted it would take just six months to build our home but it stretched into five years. He figured out ways to raise hand-crafted wooden bays by himself using a tall cedar tree, block and tackle, and a "come-along." When it came time to set the trusses and raise the roof, skilled hands of carpenters in our new community came to help. Afterwards, we celebrated with a potluck and toasts to many years of happiness in our home.

He crafted the kitchen just for me, watching as I kneaded countless loaves of bread and measuring the height of my open hands so the baking counter would be a perfect fit. A cookbook stand at just my eye level was tucked in the shelves above the counter and fishing weights dangling from monofilament line held open the books placed on it. I bought the cookstove of my dreams—a six-burner Wolf, with an oven that would easily handle two twenty-five-pound turkeys. When it was delivered, another potluck was in order, and strong friends helped to

set it in place, where it was surrounded by open shelving for dishes, pots, pans, teas, and spices. He wanted a sixth year to do all the finish work, but after five years of cabin living, I was definitely ready to move to a larger space. Father's Day and his birthday fell on the same day that year, so it was decreed as the perfect day for our housewarming party. The morning of the party, we moved in the kitchen table and chairs from the storage barn, and I broke in the new Wolf with a first pot of soup and loaves of homemade bread. This life was everything I had dreamed of and I was so grateful.

Years later as I walked with a friend around the land, she told me she had had a dream that one day she was going to live in my house. I couldn't ever imagine myself leaving, but ten years after building the house, her dream came true when I turned the keys over to her and her husband. I knew that they understood the labor of love it was to build this home, and that they would continue to care for it and love it as I did. The Wolf stove is still going strong at thirty years plus, the fishing weights still hold open cookbooks above the baking counter, and I feel so lucky that I can visit and enjoy a cup of tea in the kitchen that still remains the heart of a very special home.

How to Roast a Chicken

As a young bride, the mere thought of roasting a chicken for Sunday dinner with my in-laws was intimidating. Once I mustered up my courage and finally did it, I found that there was nothing to it. Now, I roast a bird every couple of weeks, and use the leftover meat in soups, quesadillas, sandwiches, and more. Buy chickens that are organic, free range, and sustainably and locally grown whenever possible.

SERVES 6

INGREDIENTS

One 3- to 5-pound (340-g to 2.25-kg) whole chicken

1 tablespoon coarse kosher salt

½ teaspoon freshly ground black pepper

Fresh sprigs of rosemary, sage, oregano, tarragon, or other herbs you might have

Garlic cloves (optional)

PROCEDURE

1. Preheat the oven to 350°F (180°C).
2. Pull the giblets (the heart, liver) and neck out of the cavity of the chicken, if they have been put there, and save. Sometimes you may find them in a small paper packet. Pat the bird dry.
3. Sprinkle coarse kosher salt on the inside and the outside of the bird. I probably use about a tablespoon, more or less. Grind fresh pepper all over the outside and some on the inside, too.
4. If you have fresh herbs growing in your garden, pinch off some sprigs, and tuck them into the cavity. Rosemary or sage are nice. Add the optional garlic cloves there, too. Securely wrap the legs with a piece of kitchen twine, if you have some.
5. Place the bird in an ovenproof baking dish, and bake in the preheated oven for 90 minutes. When done, a meat thermometer should read 165°F (75°C) when placed in the thickest part of the leg or breast.

Note That's all there is to it. You can occasionally baste the bird if you want, but most of the time I don't. Save the juice and drippings for soup. And those innards and neck that you saved? The neck can be used to start some chicken stock, and the liver and heart can be lightly sautéed in butter or oil for 2 minutes and added to gravy—but since I don't make gravy all that often, my sweet dog and cat get them as special treats.

Chicken Thighs Baked in a Pie

This pie filling is adapted from *Seven Centuries of English Cooking* by Maxime de la Falaise, showing us how far the Spice Trail had opened up by the fourteenth century. I think you'll find it as delicious today as it may have been in 1378. If you don't have a deep-dish pie pan, use any ovenproof baking dish.

SERVES 6 TO 8

INGREDIENTS

1 recipe Art of the Pie Dough (see page 103)

1 pound (450 g) ground pork or sausage of your choice

2 large hard-boiled eggs, roughly chopped

1 cup (100 g) grated Parmigiano-Reggiano cheese

1 tablespoon granulated sugar

1 teaspoon allspice

⅛ teaspoon saffron strands

1 teaspoon salt

4 chicken thighs, bone in and skin on, or 1 to 2 cups already cooked chicken, chopped in pieces

2 tablespoons (30 g) butter

½ cup (120 ml) chicken stock

EGG WASH

1 egg yolk plus 2 teaspoons (10 ml) water, fork beaten

PROCEDURE

1. Make the pie dough and let rest for 20 to 60 minutes in the fridge.
2. Preheat oven to 375°F (190°C).
3. In a medium bowl, mix together the pork, chopped eggs, cheese, sugar, allspice, saffron, and salt.
4. Line the bottom of a 9-inch (23-cm) deep-dish pie dish with one disc of rolled-out pie dough.
5. Add the seasoned meat mixture, and spread evenly.
6. Lightly brown the chicken thighs in butter and arrange them on top of the meat, or if using already cooked chicken, spread it evenly over the top.
7. Pour the stock over the chicken thighs or already cooked chicken meat.
8. Roll out the upper crust, and cover the filling with it. Finish the edges. Cut a few vents. Brush with egg yolk wash.
9. Bake in preheated oven for 35 to 40 minutes. Remove the pie from the oven 15 minutes into the bake, brush with egg yolk wash again, return to oven, and continue baking for 25 minutes.

Easy Cheesy Rice and Beanies

This comfort food casserole is an alternative to macaroni and cheese and one that will be appreciated by those who are no longer able to eat pasta made with gluten. Make a green salad and set the table while it's in the oven. Add a piece of seasonal fresh fruit for dessert, and your family will have enjoyed something from all of the food groups.

SERVES 6

INGREDIENTS

1 cup (200 g) short grain brown rice

2 ½ cups (600 ml) water or stock

2 tablespoon (30 g) butter or olive oil, plus more for greasing the pan

2 onions, thinly sliced

2 cloves garlic, minced

2 large eggs

1½ cups (350 ml) milk

2 teaspoons dry mustard

Small grating of nutmeg

1 teaspoon salt

1 cup (115 g) grated extra-sharp cheddar cheese,

1 cup (115 g) grated Gruyère or Swiss cheese

1 cup (100 g) grated Parmigiano-Reggiano cheese

One 15-ounce (425-g) can black beans, rinsed and drained, or 2 cups already cooked black beans

1 cup chopped chicken meat (optional)

1. In a medium-size saucepan, add rice and water or stock, and bring to a boil. Cover and reduce to a simmer. Cook until the rice has absorbed the liquid, approximately 40 minutes.
2. Once the rice is cooked, preheat oven to 375°F (190°C). Grease a square 9-inch (23-cm) ovenproof baking dish with butter or olive oil.
3. In a large skillet, melt butter or heat olive oil. Sauté onions and garlic for about 5 minutes, stirring occasionally, until onions are soft and their edges are starting to brown.
4. Mix the cheeses together. Set aside ½ cup to sprinkle on top of the casserole.
5. In a large bowl, fork beat the eggs. Stir in milk, mustard, nutmeg, and salt, and mix again.
6. Add cheese, onions, rice, beans, and optional chicken to the bowl, and mix.
7. Turn the cheesy-bean-egg mixture into the greased baking dish. Sprinkle ½ cup of cheese on top.
8. Bake in preheated oven for 40 minutes. Let it cool for about 10 minutes before serving.

Note If you have leftover rice, use about two cups, instead of cooking up a new batch. Substitute red kidney beans for black beans, and whatever cheese you have on hand such as Colby, Monterey jack, Fontina, mild cheddar, or pepper jack. For an even cheesier casserole, add more cheese to the rice and beans, and top.

Easy Cheesy Rice and Beanies, page 208

Brown Rice Casserole

I was making this one evening when my dear friend, Nancy, popped in for an unexpected visit, stayed for a bowl, asked for seconds, and the recipe, too. If you don't have the exact vegetables that are listed in the ingredients, just chop and cook whatever you *do* have on hand, and if you have some leftover cooked rice, step one is already done.

SERVES 4 TO 6

INGREDIENTS

2 cups (400 g) short grain brown rice, or enough to make 4 cups cooked

5 cups (1.2 l) water or stock

½ block (7 oz or 200 g) firm tofu, drained and patted dry, or a cup of leftover chicken, pork, beef, or fish

2 tablespoons (30 ml) olive oil

1 large onion, chopped

5 cloves garlic, minced

2 medium carrots, peeled and chopped

1 small parsnip, peeled and chopped

1 green or red pepper, chopped

6 to 8 mushrooms, roughly chopped

1 teaspoon ground cumin

Freshly ground black pepper

1 teaspoon salt

1 cup (240 ml) water or stock

¼ to ½ cup (30 to 60 g) grated cheese (cheddar, parmesan, or jack, or a combination)

1. In a medium-size saucepan, add rice and water or stock, and bring to a boil. Cover and reduce to a simmer. Cook until the rice has absorbed the liquid. This will take about 40 minutes, but longer if you pick up the lid to see if the rice is done. You can also use 4 cups of leftover rice.
2. Cut the tofu, chicken, meat, or fish into bite-size pieces and set aside.
3. Heat olive oil in large cast-iron or other frying pan. Add the onion and garlic, and cook over medium heat for about 3 minutes.
4. Add the carrots, parsnip, pepper, mushrooms, cumin, salt, pepper and ½ cup (120 ml) water or stock. Cook uncovered for 2 to 3 minutes as you stir it around a bit. Cover and cook for 5 minutes more until the vegetables soften up some. Add a little more liquid if the pan starts to get dry.
5. Preheat oven to 350°F (180°C). Mix the rice, protein, grated cheese, and remaining water or stock with the vegetable mixture. Turn into a greased casserole dish. Bake covered for 30 minutes. Remove from oven and serve.

Onion Tricks

I've read about and tried many tricks over the years that are supposed to help stop my eyes from tearing up when chopping onions: sticking a piece of bread between my teeth, cutting near steaming water, refrigerating them first, breathing through my mouth with my tongue sticking out, and even whistling while cutting. You'll have to let me know if that last one works since, try as I might, I've never been able to whistle. My solution is simple: I either cut the onion outside at a table on the deck, or by an open window so the fumes can waft away.

Macaroni and Cheese

I grew up in the era of 1950s store-bought frozen macaroni and cheese. When I had a home of my own, I happily found that homemade mac and cheese is very simple to make and so much better than what comes in a box from the freezer section. Every home cook should have a recipe for this family favorite—here's mine. If you are gluten-free, use gluten-free pasta, or take a look at Easy Cheesy Rice and Beanies (see page 208).

SERVES 6

INGREDIENTS

2 ½ cups (230 g) uncooked macaroni—this will make about 5 cups cooked

2 cups (450 ml) milk, half and half, or a combination

½ teaspoon salt

⅛ teaspoon freshly ground black pepper

1 heaping teaspoon dry mustard

3 ½ cups grated extra sharp cheddar cheese, plus ½ cup to top the casserole (425 g total)

PROCEDURE

1. Preheat the oven to 350°F (180°C). Grease an ovenproof casserole with butter.
2. Cook the macaroni until still slightly firm according to the directions on the package. Drain and set aside.
3. In a large bowl, mix the milk or half and half, salt, pepper, and mustard.
4. Add the macaroni and 3 cups cheese to the bowl, and mix.
5. Turn into the greased casserole. Top with remaining ½ cup of grated cheese.
6. Bake in the preheated oven for 35 to 40 minutes until it's nice and bubbly on top.

Note Feel free to use a mix of other cheeses you have on hand. If you like it even cheesier, add more cheese to the macaroni, and on the top.

Duncan's Pizza

My son, Duncan, has turned into a very competent pizza maker. New York friends, who are always the first to critique a pizza for authenticity, have said that his is top notch, which is no small feat. As for toppings, at Pie Cottage, they are always an improvisational affair and can be simple or multi-layered. It doesn't take much yeast for this dough: one teaspoon, or about a half a packet, works here. After swishing it around in warm water with the sweetener, you'll know if your yeast is active when you see what looks like little fireworks going off in the water. This is called the bloom, and it tells us that the "yeasty-beasties," the name we gave to them when Duncan was a little boy, are alive and multiplying. If you don't see any activity after 5 minutes, the water may have been too hot, or the yeast not fresh.

2 PIZZAS

INGREDIENTS

1 tablespoon honey or granulated sugar

1½ cups (350 ml) lukewarm water (about the temperature of your skin)

1 teaspoon dry active yeast

¼ cup (60 ml) olive oil, plus ½ teaspoon (120 ml) olive oil for bowl

½ teaspoon salt

2 tablespoons Italian or pizza seasoning, or a combination of individual spices and seasonings, such as powdered onion, garlic, oregano, thyme, salt, and freshly ground black pepper

3 ½ cups (510 g) unbleached all-purpose flour, plus ¼ cup (35 g) for rolling out dough

DOUGH

1. In a large mixing bowl, mix sugar or honey into the lukewarm water.
2. Add yeast and stir until dissolved. Wait until you see the yeast start to bloom.
3. Stir in olive oil, salt, and optional Italian or pizza seasoning.
4. Add 2 cups (290 g) flour and mix in completely with a spoon or fork. The mixture will be very sticky.
5. Evenly spread the remaining 1½ cups (220 g) flour on top of the sticky dough, but do not mix in.
6. Place your open hands on top of the dough, and, with your fingers gently curled under the edge farthest from you, lift the dough and turn it over several times so it is covered with flour. Toss a bit more extra flour under the bottom of the dough, too.

7. Once the dough is completely covered in flour, knead the dough in the bowl. About 10 to 15 times should do. There will be some left-over flour. The dough will feel slightly moist but not sticky. If it is sticky and all over your hands, knead in a bit more flour.
8. Shape the dough into a ball, and let rest on the counter while you clean out the bowl.
9. Coat the bottom and sides of the bowl with ½ teaspoon olive oil to prevent the dough from sticking later.
10. Place dough in bowl, cover with a cloth, and let rise for 2 hours, or until double in size.
11. About 10 minutes before you are ready to roll the dough, place a pizza stone (if you have one) in the oven, and preheat to 500°F (260°C)

ROLLING OUT THE DOUGH, CONSTRUCTING, AND BAKING THE PIZZA

1. Sprinkle about ¼ cup (35 g) flour on a moveable flat surface such as a breadboard or pizza peel.
2. Cut the dough in two equal parts and place one on the floured surface. Re-cover the remaining dough. Coat both sides of the dough you are rolling with flour so it won't stick.
3. Roll out the dough to approximately a 14- to 16-inch (35- to 40-cm) circle or desired shape, and about ¼-inch (5-mm) thick.
4. Fold the dough in half and sprinkle a generous amount of flour on the board. Unfold the dough on top of the flour. Repeat with the other side so that the entire dough has a layer of flour under it and won't stick when it slides onto the pizza stone or cookie tin in step 8. You can also use semolina flour or cornmeal.
5. Fold up towards the center about 2 inches (5 cm) of the edge of the dough. An optional step is to add some cheese on the edge of the dough and roll the pizza dough over it.
6. Before you add the toppings, make sure the dough can move freely on the rolling surface. If it doesn't, repeat step 4.
7. Add sauce and toppings of choice (see below).
8. Slide the pizza onto the heated pizza stone, or onto an unheated cookie tin.
9. Bake in the preheated oven for 10 to 15 minutes or until the cheese is bubbly and golden.
10. Remove from oven and let rest a few minutes before slicing and serving.

CONTINUED

Some Ideas for Sauces

Choose a sauce and spread on top of rolled-out pizza dough. About ½ cup (120 ml) should do. Some suggestions are:

Marinara • Pesto (page 149) • BBQ • Alfredo

Tomato sauce can be a little thin, so thicken it with some tomato paste.
It will give a richer flavor, too.

Some Ideas for Toppings

Add toppings of your choice evenly over the top of the sauce. Here are a few suggestions, but let your imagination run wild.

Grated cheese (mozzarella, parmesan, sharp cheddar, jack,
or pepper jack, feta, goat, blue cheese, or a combination)

Sliced mushrooms • Sliced green peppers • Sliced black olives

Thinly sliced onions • Minced garlic • Marinated artichoke hearts

Chopped jalapeño peppers • Pineapple chunks

Mama Lil's Marinated Red Peppers, or other marinated red peppers

Sliced or diced fresh tomatoes • Spinach leaves • Basil leaves

Sliced pepperoni • Sliced salami • Chopped ham

Cooked and crumbled bacon • Cooked and crumbled sausage

Cooked and chopped chicken • Roasted tomatoes (see page 150)

Roasted garlic (see page 132) • Anchovies

Roasted Brussels sprouts (see Brussels, Bacon, and Blue on page 139)

Sliced roasted root vegetables (see page 120)

Pizza Night We all loved pizza night, where we joined friends for another once-a-month get-together. Twenty, forty, and, on one occasion almost eighty friends of all ages, gathered for what became a much-anticipated evening of conversation and good food. Our hosts made the dough and heated up their homemade wood-fired pizza oven earlier in the day; the rest of us brought toppings, sides, wine, and desserts. We rolled out our pizzas and popped them in the oven while the kids played or, as they got older, made an appearance with the current boy- or girlfriends. Living rurally, gatherings like these are a great way to catch up on all the latest news and goings on.

Spinach Lasagna

This vegetarian lasagna is a nice alternative to a traditional red sauce and meat version. It satisfies hungry teenagers, too.

INGREDIENTS

2 pounds (900 g) small curd cottage cheese or ricotta cheese

2 large eggs, fork beaten

1 tablespoon chopped parsley

Salt and freshly ground black pepper

½ cup (115 ml) melted butter

¼ teaspoon garlic powder

1 pound (450 g) fresh or frozen spinach, cooked, drained, squeezed, and chopped

1 pound (450 g) package lasagna noodles

1 pound (450 g) grated Monterey jack cheese

1 cup (100 g) grated Parmigiano-Reggiano cheese

PROCEDURE

1. Preheat oven to 350°F (180°C). Grease a 12-by-15-inch (30-by-38-cm) ovenproof baking dish or something of similar size.
2. In a large bowl, mix together cottage or ricotta cheese, eggs, parsley, salt, pepper, and butter.
3. Add garlic powder to the cooked spinach, and mix with a fork a bit to spread it through evenly.
4. Cook lasagna noodles following the directions on the package, drain, and rinse so they don't stick together. If using no-cook, add an extra cup of water to the pan before making the lasagna layers.
5. Add layers into the greased baking dish in this order: noodles, cottage cheese mixture, Monterey jack, Parmigiano-Reggiano, and spinach. Repeat the layers again.
6. Bake in the oven for 35 to 40 minutes until bubbly.

Meaty Lasagna

In my teens, I dated a boy who, a decade later, would become my first wuzband. With five brothers and sisters, his home was always hopping with activity. His mom loved to cook and I was often invited to share their family table, which is a good way to get to know with whom your kids are spending time. This adaption of her lasagna recipe uses either cooked or no-cook noodles. As a busy mom in the 1960s, and had the time-saving no-cook variety been available, I imagine she would have been one of the first to place them into her shopping cart.

SERVES 6 TO 8

INGREDIENTS

2 tablespoons (30 ml) olive oil

2 to 4 cloves garlic, minced

1 pound (450 g) ground beef, or a combination of ground beef and mild Italian sausage

Two 15-ounce cans (850 g total) tomato sauce

½ teaspoon salt

¼ teaspoon freshly ground black pepper

½ teaspoon dried oregano

8 ounces (225 g) lasagna noodles

½ pound (225 g) mozzarella cheese

½ cup (50 g) grated Parmigiano-Reggiano cheese

One 15-ounce (425-g) carton ricotta cheese

CONTINUED

1. Preheat oven to 375°F (190°C).
2. In a large cast-iron skillet or sauté pan, heat the olive oil over medium-low heat. Add garlic and let cook for about 30 seconds. Add the meat and cook for 5 minutes until browned. While cooking, break the meat up with a spoon into medium and small pieces. Turn on often to make sure that all sides are browned. Drain any extra fat off.
3. Add tomato sauce, salt, pepper, and oregano to the meat. Cover and simmer for 15 minutes.
4. Cook lasagna noodles following the directions on the package, drain, and rinse so they don't stick together. If using no-cook noodles, stir in an extra cup of water to the sauce before making the lasagna layers.
5. Place ½ cup sauce in a 13-by-9-inch (33x-by-22-cm) ovenproof baking dish or another dish of approximate size, and spread around evenly.
6. Add layers into the baking dish in this order: noodles, mozzarella, Parmigiano-Reggiano, ricotta, and tomato-meat sauce. Repeat the layers again.
7. Bake in the preheated oven for 35 to 40 minutes until bubbly.

Veggie Mex Casserole

I had a field day opening up all the different spices jars on my shelves when I first made this casserole. If you find it easiest to use a heaping tablespoon of a Mexican seasoning, to take the place of the oregano, basil, cumin, and coriander, that's fine, too. Either way you do it, it is a delicious casserole that makes a nice potluck dish, and the leftovers are good reheated, too.

SERVES 6 WITH SOME EXTRA FOR TOMORROW'S LUNCH

INGREDIENTS

4 large eggs

1½ cups (340 g) sour cream or plain yogurt, plus more for serving

1 cup (115 g) grated pepper jack cheese

1 cup (115 g) grated extra sharp cheddar

2 tablespoons (30 ml) olive oil

8 cloves garlic, minced

2 medium onions, chopped in ¼- to ½-inch (5- to 10-ml) pieces

1 teaspoon dried oregano

1 teaspoon dried basil

1 teaspoon ground cumin

½ teaspoon ground coriander

½ teaspoon dry mustard

⅛ teaspoon cayenne

1 green pepper, diced

2 cups (130 g) sliced mushrooms

One 15-ounce (425-g) can crushed tomatoes, or 3 medium tomatoes, diced

One 15.5-ounce (439-g) can organic corn

½ cup fresh minced parsley

1 teaspoon salt

Dash of paprika

Salsa, for serving

Tasty Guacamole (see page 59), for serving

1. Preheat the oven to 375°F (190°C). Grease a 9-by-13-inch (23-by-33-cm) ovenproof baking dish.

2. In a medium bowl, beat the eggs and sour cream or yogurt, and set aside.

3. Mix the cheeses, and set aside.

4. In a large cast-iron skillet or sauté pan, heat the olive oil over medium-low heat. Add the garlic and onions. Add the oregano, basil, cumin, and coriander, or 1 heaping tablespoon of Mexican seasoning. Add the mustard and cayenne, and sauté for about 5 minutes until the onions start to wilt and brown along their edges.

5. Add the peppers and cook for 2 minutes. Add the mushrooms and cook for 2 minutes more.

6. Put a large colander or a sieve strainer over a bowl. Turn the cooked mixture into the colander, and allow any extra liquid to drip through. Discard the liquid, and turn the drained vegetables into the bowl.

7. Add the tomatoes, corn, parsley, and salt, and mix well.

8. Spread half of the vegetables in the greased ovenproof baking dish, and half of the mixed cheeses on top of that. Repeat with the remaining half of the vegetables. Top with the remaining layer of mixed cheeses.

9. Pour the egg mix as evenly as possible over the top. Sprinkle with a little paprika.

10. Bake in preheated oven covered with foil for 30 minutes. Remove the foil, return to oven, and bake for an additional 10 minutes, or until the top is golden.

11. Remove from oven, and let cool while you set the table. Serve with extra sour cream or plain yogurt, salsa, and guacamole.

Tortilla Casserole

Corn tortillas, cheese, onions, garlic, and tomatoes, either canned or fresh, are staples at Pie Cottage. I think the list is probably a holdover from growing up in Southern California where I learned to make satisfying breakfasts, lunches, and dinners with them. This casserole uses a little heavy cream, but if it means a trip to the grocery store for just that one thing, it's okay to use half and half, or milk. As for cheeses, I like a combination of Parmigiano-Reggiano and jack, but I've made it with sharp cheddar, too.

SERVES 4 TO 6

INGREDIENTS

Ten 6-inch (15-cm) corn tortillas

2 tablespoons (30 ml) olive oil

1 clove garlic, minced

1 medium onion, chopped small

One 15-ounce (425-g) can crushed tomatoes, or 3 medium tomatoes, peeled, seeded, and chopped

1 teaspoon oregano

½ teaspoon granulated sugar

½ teaspoon salt

⅛ teaspoon freshly ground black pepper

½ cup (120 ml) heavy cream

½ cup (50 g) grated Parmigiano-Reggiano cheese

½ cup (55 g) grated jack cheese

Chopped cilantro or parsley, for serving

Pickled red peppers in oil, for serving

PROCEDURE

1. Preheat oven to 350°F (180°C).
2. Cut tortillas into 3-by-½-inch (7.5-by-1-cm) strips.
3. In a large saucepan, heat the olive oil over medium-low heat. Add the garlic and onion and sauté until the onion is soft and translucent.
4. Add tomatoes, oregano, sugar, salt, and pepper. Raise heat, bring to a boil, and then turn down to low.
5. Fold in tortilla strips, heavy cream, and Parmigiano-Reggiano. Remove from heat.
6. Turn into an ungreased 1-quart casserole. Bake uncovered for 30 minutes.
7. Remove from oven, and sprinkle with jack cheese. Return to oven for 2 to 3 minutes more to melt the cheese.
8. Garnish with freshly chopped cilantro or parsley and red peppers.

Black Bean and Meat of Your Choice Enchiladas

I learned to make enchiladas in my hometown of Santa Barbara, where everybody's mom, auntie, and grandmother had a favorite way to make them. The most traditional way I learned is to first dip corn tortillas in sauce and then soften them in heated oil, which is how I've described it for you in the steps here. You can also fry them in hot oil to soften first, and dip them in sauce afterward. Either way you do it, be prepared to wipe up some spatters. To avoid that spattery mess, make Enchilada Casserole, the Easy Way (see page 229), which is layered like lasagna.

SERVES 4 TO 6

INGREDIENTS

Canola or safflower oil for frying

One 19-ounce (538-g) can green or red enchilada sauce

Twelve 6-inch (15-cm) corn tortillas

One 15-ounce (425-g) can black beans, drained

2 cups (230 g) grated cheese, a combination of jack and sharp cheddar

Leftover chicken, pork, or beef, chopped into bite-size pieces (optional)

1 onion, chopped small

One 2.25-ounce (64-g) can sliced ripe black olives

One 4-ounce (113-g) can diced green chilies

Sour cream, for serving

Salsa, for serving

Tasty Guacamole (see page 59), for serving

PROCEDURE

1. Preheat oven to 350°F (180°C).
2. Place 1 inch (2.5 cm) of oil in a frying pan, and heat to medium hot.
3. Put some of the enchilada sauce in a pie pan or square cake pan. Use tongs, dip one tortilla at a time into the sauce to coat both sides. Place the coated tortilla into the hot oil for a few seconds until it softens. Using tongs, immediately remove from oil and place on a plate to drain.
4. Repeat step 3 until all tortillas are softened and stacked on the plate.
5. Take one softened tortilla, place it in a large ovenproof baking dish, and fill with 2 tablespoons black beans, 1 tablespoon cheese, 1 to 2 tablespoons optional meat, 1 tablespoon onion, 1 teaspoon olives, and 1 teaspoon green chilies.

6. Roll the tortilla around the filling, making sure the overlapped flap is underneath. Repeat steps 5 and 6 until all the tortillas are used and the baking dish is filled.
7. Pour extra sauce over the top of the enchiladas.
8. Top with a sprinkling of grated cheese, and any remaining olives or chilies.
9. Bake in the preheated oven uncovered for 25 to 30 minutes until heated through, and cheese on top has melted.
10. Serve with sour cream, salsa, and guacamole.

Enchilada Casserole, the Easy Way

This casserole uses all the ingredients from the enchiladas above except for the oil, and you won't have any spattery mess. Use tortillas and layer it like a lasagna.

PROCEDURE

1. Preheat oven to 350°F (180°C).
2. In a square 8-inch (20-cm) baking dish or other casserole of about the same size, pour ¼ cup red or green enchilada sauce and spread around so it is distributed evenly.
3. Cover with 4 corn tortillas, overlapping as necessary.
4. Layer on top half the beans and meat, and one third of the onions, black olives, green chilies, and cheese.
5. Repeat steps 3 and 4.
6. Place a final layer of 4 tortillas on top, overlapping as necessary.
7. Pour remaining red or green enchilada sauce over the top.
8. Evenly sprinkle on top the remaining grated cheese, onions, olives, and peppers. If you like even more cheese, add it now.
9. Bake in preheated oven uncovered for 25 to 30 minutes until heated through and cheese on top has melted.
10. Serve with sour cream, salsa, and guacamole.

Duncan's Fish Tacos

Meals at Pie Cottage are always informal affairs, and taco night is especially so. In addition to the fish, we make a host of fixings and place them on the counter to fill our tortillas—Spicy Slaw (see page 233), Spanish Rice (see page 234), Seasoned Black Beans (see page 235), and Tasty Guacamole (see page 59). You can make as many or as few of the fixings as you like, but these tacos are really good when all are available.

MAKES 10 TO 12 TACOS

INGREDIENTS

¼ teaspoon salt

¼ teaspoon freshly ground black pepper

¼ teaspoon paprika

¼ teaspoon herb of choice such as thyme, marjoram, or dill (optional)

1 pound (450 g) fish filets such as rockfish, halibut, cod, or salmon

Ten to twelve 6-inch (15-cm) corn or flour tortillas

1 teaspoon olive oil

Grated Monterey jack cheese

Chopped cilantro

Salsa or hot sauce of choice

Lime wedges

Spicy Slaw (see page 233), for serving

Spanish Rice (see page 234), for serving

Seasoned Black Beans (see page 235), for serving

Tasty Guacamole (see page 59), for serving

CONTINUED

1. Mix together the salt, pepper, paprika, and optional herb. Sprinkle the herb mix evenly over the fish. Preheat oven to 225°F (110°C).

2. Place a large frying pan over high heat. When the pan is hot, add the olive oil.

3. Add the fish filets, and sear about 1 minute on each side. Reduce heat to medium, cover, and continue cooking for about 3 minutes. Check the thickest part of the filet to see if it is cooked all the way through. If not, continue cooking for another minute. Cooking time will vary depending on thickness of filets.

4. Remove pan from heat. Place filets on a platter, and use a fork to break up some of the larger pieces so they are easy to fit into the tortillas. Cover, and set in preheated oven to stay warm while softening the tortillas.

5. To soften the tortillas, stack five on a microwavable plate, cover with a damp paper towel, and microwave for 20-second increments until soft. You can also wrap a stack of five in aluminum foil, and heat in a 350°F (180°C) oven for about 15 minutes. Either way, their own steam will soften them. Place warm softened tortillas on a plate, and cover with another plate so they won't dry out.

6. Set the tortillas, fish, grated cheese, cilantro, salsa, and lime wedges on the counter or table.

7. Fill each tortilla with some of everything. Squeeze some lime juice over the top of each taco.

8. Serve with Spicy Slaw, Spanish Rice, Seasoned Black Beans, and Tasty Guacamole.

Spicy Slaw

Duncan makes this salad to serve with his fish tacos (see page 231). There's usually some left over to enjoy with sandwiches, or tucked into a Stuffed Pita (see page 68). For a non-spicy version, leave out the jalapeño.

SERVES 6 TO 8

INGREDIENTS

½ small green cabbage, shredded (about 4 cups)

½ small red cabbage, shredded (about 4 cups)

2 medium carrots, grated

3 scallions, whites and greens, thinly sliced

½ to 1 whole jalapeño, seeded and minced (optional)

½ large yellow onion, diced

DRESSING

3 cloves garlic, minced

1 tablespoon (15 g) freshly squeezed lime juice

2 tablespoons mayonnaise

1 tablespoon granulated sugar or honey, or to taste

Salt and freshly ground black pepper

1 teaspoon dried dill

PROCEDURE

1. Place the shredded cabbage, carrots, scallions, optional jalapeño, and onion in a large bowl and mix well.
2. Place the garlic, lime juice, mayonnaise, sugar or honey, salt, pepper, and dill into a jar with a lid and shake well. Pour the dressing over the slaw, and toss until well coated.
3. Cover and refrigerate for 1 hour before serving.

Spanish Rice

This easy rice is great to serve with Fish Tacos (see page 231), Tortilla Casserole (see page 227), or Enchiladas (see page 228). When there's extra, I stuff it in peppers or pita, or serve with eggs.

INGREDIENTS

2 teaspoons (10 ml) olive oil

½ medium yellow onion, chopped

2 cloves garlic, minced

1 medium carrot, diced

1 cup (200 g) white rice, uncooked

1¾ cups (425 ml) chicken stock

1 tablespoon tomato paste

1 teaspoon salt

¼ teaspoon freshly ground black pepper

PROCEDURE

1. Heat oil in a large cast-iron pan over medium heat. Add chopped onion and cook until just starting to turn translucent.
2. Add garlic and carrot, and cook for 5 minutes, stirring occasionally.
3. Add rice, chicken stock, tomato paste, salt, and pepper. Stir to combine tomato paste with the stock. Continue to stir occasionally while you bring the liquid to a boil. Reduce heat to medium-low, and cover. Simmer until stock is absorbed. Check at about 15 minutes.
4. Remove from heat, and let sit, covered, for at least 5 minutes. Fluff rice with a fork, and serve.

Seasoned Black Beans

Add a few spices to canned black beans for a quick pot of beans that can be served at any meal. These are our favorite beans to serve with Duncan's Fish Tacos (see page 231).

SERVES 2 TO 3

INGREDIENTS

1 tablespoon (15 ml) olive oil

One 15.5-ounce (434-g) can black beans, rinsed and drained

½ teaspoon garlic powder

½ teaspoon chili powder or smoked chili powder

½ teaspoon ground cumin

½ teaspoon salt

PROCEDURE

1. Place olive oil in a saucepan over medium-low heat. Add the black beans, garlic powder, chili powder, cumin, and salt, and stir. Reduce heat to low and cook for about 5 to 10 minutes or until heated through. Add a little water if the beans become too dry.
2. Mash slightly with the back of a spoon, remove from heat, and serve.

Steamed Manila Clams with Garlic

A delicious meal with Manila clams can be on the table in a jiffy. For a hungry crowd, cook up a package of pasta, and pour the clams, with their shells and juice, right over the top.

SERVES 4 TO 6

INGREDIENTS

2 tablespoons (30 g) butter

2 tablespoons (30 ml) olive oil

6 cloves garlic, minced

4 to 5 pounds (1.8 to 2.25 kg) Manila Clams, rinsed well

1 cup white wine or vermouth (optional)

1 scallion, greens only, thinly sliced, for garnish

Slices of rustic Italian bread, for serving

PROCEDURE

1. In a large pan with a fitted lid, heat the butter and olive oil over medium heat.
2. Add the garlic and let brown lightly. Stir as you cook it so it doesn't burn.
3. Add rinsed clams and optional wine or vermouth. Stir to mix, and cover tightly.
4. Turn the heat up to high, bring to boil, and cook. Lift the lid after 5 minutes to see if the shells have opened. Return the lid and continue cooking until the majority of shells are open.
5. Sprinkle scallions on top, cover, and cook for another minute.
6. Serve with crusty bread to sop up the delicious juice.

Note Be sure to buy clams that are tightly shut. Discard any that are open, dry looking, and do not smell fresh.

Super Easy Mussels, Garlic, and Bread

I've cooked up mussels at picnics over a propane burner and even a beach campfire. Mediterranean mussels are ready during the summer when the tomatoes are ripe. A salad of sliced tomatoes, drizzled with olive oil, seasoned with salt and pepper, and finished with a light sprinkling of freshly chopped basil is my idea of Northwest heaven. As with all shellfish, discard any that are open, dry looking, or do not smell fresh.

SERVES 4

INGREDIENTS

1½ to 2 pounds (675 to 900 g) Mediterranean mussels

3 cloves garlic, coarsely chopped

A handful or two fresh parsley, coarsely chopped

Freshly ground black pepper, to taste

Slices of rustic Italian bread, for serving

PROCEDURE

1. De-beard and rinse mussels. Discard the beards.
2. Place a large cast-iron skillet or pan over high heat. When the skillet is smoking hot, add the mussels, and cover immediately. You will hear a sizzle sound when you add them.
3. Shake the covered pan every once in awhile. Cook until the mussel shells have opened. Stir in the garlic and parsley, cover, and let them cook another minute or two.
4. Season with some freshly ground black pepper, and serve with slices of grilled rustic Italian bread to soak up the juices.

Note To debeard mussels, tug and pull out the little strings that hang out of the mussel shell. Discard the strings.

Uncle Alphonso's No-Fuss Paella

I have known Renée all my life. She called my dad Uncle Hershey because of all the Hershey bars that he would bring to her family on Christmas, Easter, and birthdays. Renée attended college in Spain, and met and later married a Spaniard who serenaded her below her balcony. It all sounded so romantic. On her visits back to Santa Barbara, our families always got together, and she made the delicious paella she had learned in Spain from her husband's Uncle Alphonso. I still have my handwritten index card with this recipe, and at the top I wrote just two words: "Yum Yum!"

SERVES 6

INGREDIENTS

- 2 tablespoons (30 g) olive oil
- 1 whole chicken, cut in pieces or 2 ½ to 3 pounds (1 to 1.3 kg) chicken thighs—skin on will brown best
- 6 cloves garlic, sliced
- 1 medium onion, chopped
- 1 green pepper, chopped
- 1 or 2 large ripe tomatoes, chopped
- 1 tablespoon chopped fresh or dried parsley
- 1½ teaspoons salt
- 1 good-sized pinch saffron, about 20 strands (mash a little with the back of a spoon)
- 1 cup (130 g) peas, fresh or frozen
- ½ cup (120 g) pitted black or green olives
- 2 cups (400 g white rice, uncooked
- 5 cups (1.2 l) chicken stock
- 1 pound (450 g) prawns or large shrimp of your choice, peeled and deveined shrimp (optional)

1. In a large cast-iron skillet or pan, heat the olive oil over medium heat. Sauté the chicken pieces for 3 to 4 minutes on each side until light golden brown. Remove from pan, drain on paper towels, or put in strainer to let the extra oil drip through. Set aside.
2. Turn the heat to low under the pan, add more olive oil if needed, add the garlic and onion, and sauté for about 5 minutes until the onion is brown on the edges. Stir occasionally.
3. Add green pepper, and cook for 3 minutes. Add the tomato, and cook for 3 to 4 minutes, stirring occasionally.
4. Add the parsley, salt, mashed saffron, peas, and olives, and stir gently to mix.
5. Stir in the rice and stock. Bring to a boil.
6. Reduce heat to simmer, cook for 15 minutes.
7. Add pieces of chicken, and optional shrimp. Continue cooking for another 15 to 20 minutes. Turn the shrimp over occasionally, or bury them deeper into the rice. Add more chicken stock as needed.
8. When the rice is soft and the liquid is absorbed, the paella is ready.

Note

You can add chorizo or hot or sweet Italian sausage. Cut into pieces and pan-fry, and then add to the paella when you add the chicken. I use saffron from Trader Joe's for this recipe.

Uncle Alphonso's No-Fuss Paella, page 240

Simple Seared Salmon with Braised Balsamic Greens and Garlic, page 244

Simple Seared Salmon with Braised Balsamic Greens and Garlic

This must be the easiest and most foolproof way to cook salmon ever. It works just as well for halibut. The fish is seared quickly in a hot skillet to seal the juices in, and finished off in a low-temperature oven. Made this way, it is virtually impossible to overcook. While it's in the oven, you will have time to braise the greens, set the table, and pour the wine. Be sure to buy wild and not farm-raised salmon. There is a difference in flavor. Balsamic vinegars are not all alike either, and can vary in flavor and quality, so get the best you can afford.

SIMPLE SEARED SALMON

½ pound (225 g) salmon steak for each person

Olive oil

Salt and freshly ground black pepper

PROCEDURE

1. Preheat oven to 225 to 250°F (110 to 120°C).
2. Brush both sides of each piece of fish with olive oil, and sprinkle with some salt and pepper.
3. Heat cast-iron skillet over medium-high heat until water dances on the surface when a few drops are sprinkled on top.
4. Sear steaks for 20 seconds on each side. I sear the flesh side, and then flip it over so that the skin side is on the bottom when it goes into the oven. If it is a thick piece, be sure to sear the cut sides, too.
5. Place skillet in the preheated oven for approximately 15 minutes. You'll know when the salmon is done when you see a tiny bit of the white albumin peeking through the flakes of the fish.
6. Cook up the braised greens while the fish is cooking (recipe below).
7. Place some braised greens on each plate, and top with a salmon steak.

1 to 2 bunches greens, such as kale, collard greens, or chard

2 tablespoons (30 ml) olive oil

3 to 6 cloves garlic, roughly chopped

Salt and freshly ground black pepper

2 to 3 tablespoons (30 to 45 ml) balsamic vinegar

PROCEDURE

1. Remove the leaves from the tough ribs of the greens. Chop or tear the greens into small- and medium-size pieces.
2. In a large cast-iron skillet or sauté pan, heat the olive oil over medium-low heat.
3. Add the garlic and sauté for a minute or so while stirring. Be careful not to burn the garlic.
4. Add the greens, and stir around to coat them with the oil. Cover the pan and let cook for a few minutes until the greens have wilted. A tightly fitted piece of foil will do just fine if you don't have a lid.
5. Season with salt and pepper.
6. Pour the balsamic vinegar over the greens and toss lightly to mix.

Afterword:
Some Thoughts for the Way

I used to think that I had travelled many roads in my life, but now, in my mid-sixties, I see that there has been just one path with many surprising twists and unexpected turns. It has given me once-in-a-lifetime opportunities to experience love and happiness, as well as sadness and sorrow.

My dream had been to marry, live in a big happy home with a houseful of children . . . six seemed the perfect number . . . and that each day would be full of cooking, baking, reading, gardening, dancing, music, mischief, and magic. At our big table, there would always be room for one more. That dream came true, but not quite in the way I thought it would. I married, but it was more than once. I built the big house and called it home, until it was time to pass it on. Though there were not six children, there were two whom I will love forever with all my heart . . . and at my table, there is always room for one more.

It would be nice if life came with an instruction manual, but since it doesn't, we spend our days learning, so we can write our own. Below are a few thoughts from my own personal help pages, and ones that that continue to help me along the way. Maybe you'll find them useful, too.

Take the next step and keep going.

Enjoy the journey as you may only pass this way once.

Find meaningful work to do.

It's okay not to know the answer.

Learn from your failures.

Ask for help when you need it.

Celebrate your successes.

Take time to play.

Have a sense of humor.

Let go of grudges as quickly as possible.

The only person you can fix is yourself.

Treat each person as you would like to be treated, with kindness, courtesy, generosity, and respect.

Love will always prevail.

Thanks for sharing my table.

Acknowledgments

The team that I am privileged to work with a second time is beyond anything that I could have dreamed to be possible. Although I wrote the words and recipes, once again "Team Pie" has brought them to life on these pages. My deepest gratitude to my editor, Ann Treistman; agent, Joy Tutela; photographer, Andrew Scrivani; book designer, Nick Caruso; publicity & marketing manager, Devorah Backman; and publicist, Megan Swartz Gellert. From the bottom of my heart, thank you for your combined vision, dedication, talent, and care.

To the team in Port Angeles, Washington that helped to make the Pie Cottage portion of the photo shoot so smooth and fun; Leigh Olson for props, styling, videos, and whiskey, Cindy Erickson for extra hands and calming presence in the kitchen, and as always, my wonderful son, Duncan, who is one of the kindest people I know. I am so lucky you are my son.

Many thanks to Judy Amster-Burton for your friendship and words, Lance and Annetta Callin-Young for pizza nights, Kathi and Bob Pressley for letting me enjoy the comforts of my old kitchen and cabin, Nancy Rivers for standing strong with me through both the rough times and good times, and Bonnie and Larry Hurd for your selfless devotion to Sara.

To Debi Koenig for "Mary Poppins" cookies and opening your home to me, and Jane Bonacci for your generous heart and wheels when needed. Many thanks to Laura and Stewart Wilson for gin and tonics and always providing a pillow when needed, Renee Castagnola for being a part of my life since I was a baby and sharing paella with my family, Greg Atkinson for friendship and the best granola recipe, Lily Athair for beautiful Morel Compass mushrooms, Bill and Betsy Taylor for friendship and shellfish, Kim and Ciro Pasciuto for generosity and passion, and to Maggie Finefrock, who continues to unfailingly challenge and inspire me to take the next step always.

A big thank you and hug to the loyal followers of the Art of the Pie blog and newsletter. This book is for you.

I would not be who I am without the love and devoted care of those who came before; my father, Thomas Joseph McDermott; my mother, Helen Louise McDermott Voorhees; my grandmother, Vesta Marie "Geeg" Jackson; beloved Sadie Flynn; and most especially my sweet daughter, Sara Elaine Phillips. I carry all of you with me in my heart each and every day.

A final thank you to Hestia, the goddess of the hearth, whose flame burns true and bright.

Credits:
Kate McDermott, Author/Food Stylist
Andrew Scrivani, Photographer
Leigh Olsen, Prop Stylist, Port Angeles
Duncan Graham, Food Stylist Assistant, Port Angeles
Cindy Erickson, Food Stylist Assistant, Port Angeles

Index

Italics are used to indicate illustrations.